DOROTHY of OZ™ Prequel

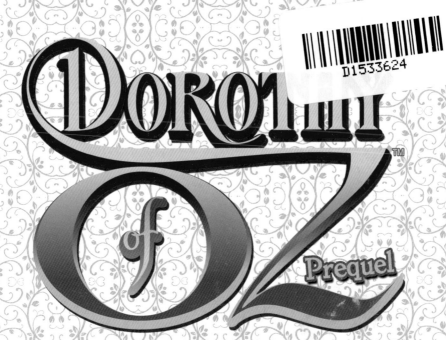

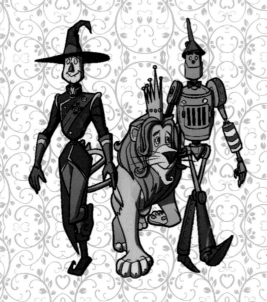

Dorothy of Oz Prequel

⌖ Cover by ⌖
Eric Shanower

⌖ Cover Colors by ⌖
Joana Lafuente

⌖ Collection Edits by ⌖
**Justin Eisinger
& Alonzo Simon**

⌖ Collection Design by ⌖
Tom B. Long

Special thanks to Travis Rutherford, Kirsti Tichenor, and Summertime Entertainment.

IDW founded by Ted Adams, Alex Garner, Kris Oprisko, and Robbie Robbins | ISBN: 978-1-61377-217-1

www.DOROTHYOFOZ.com

15 14 13 12 1 2 3 4

Ted Adams, CEO & Publisher
Greg Goldstein, President & COO
Robbie Robbins, EVP/Sr. Graphic Artist
Chris Ryall, Chief Creative Officer/Editor-in-Chief
Matthew Ruzicka, CPA, Chief Financial Officer
Alan Payne, VP of Sales
Dirk Wood, VP of Marketing
Lorelei Bunjes, VP of Digital Services

Become our fan on Facebook **facebook.com/idwpublishing**
Follow us on Twitter **@idwpublishing**
Check us out on YouTube **youtube.com/idwpublishing**
www.IDWPUBLISHING.com

The Jester and the Magic Scepter

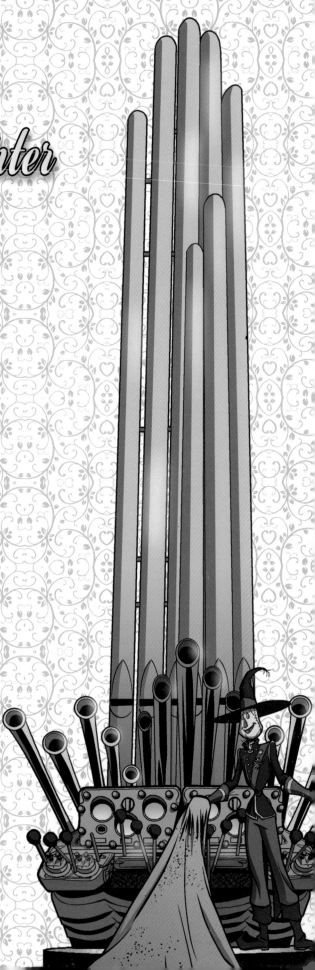

Written by
Denton J. Tipton

Art by
Blair Shedd

Colors by
Joana Lafuente

Letters by
**Neil Uyetake,
Shawn Lee,
& Chris Mowry**

Series Edits by
Denton J. Tipton

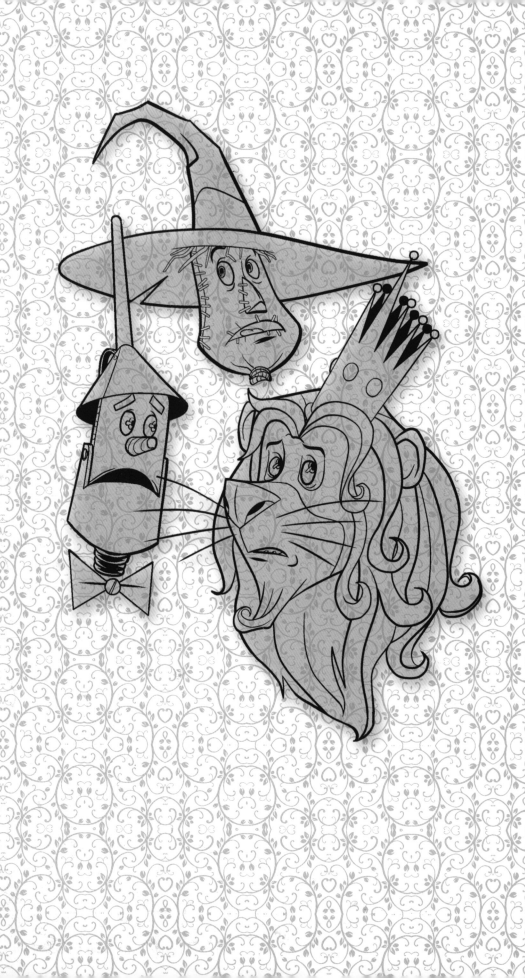

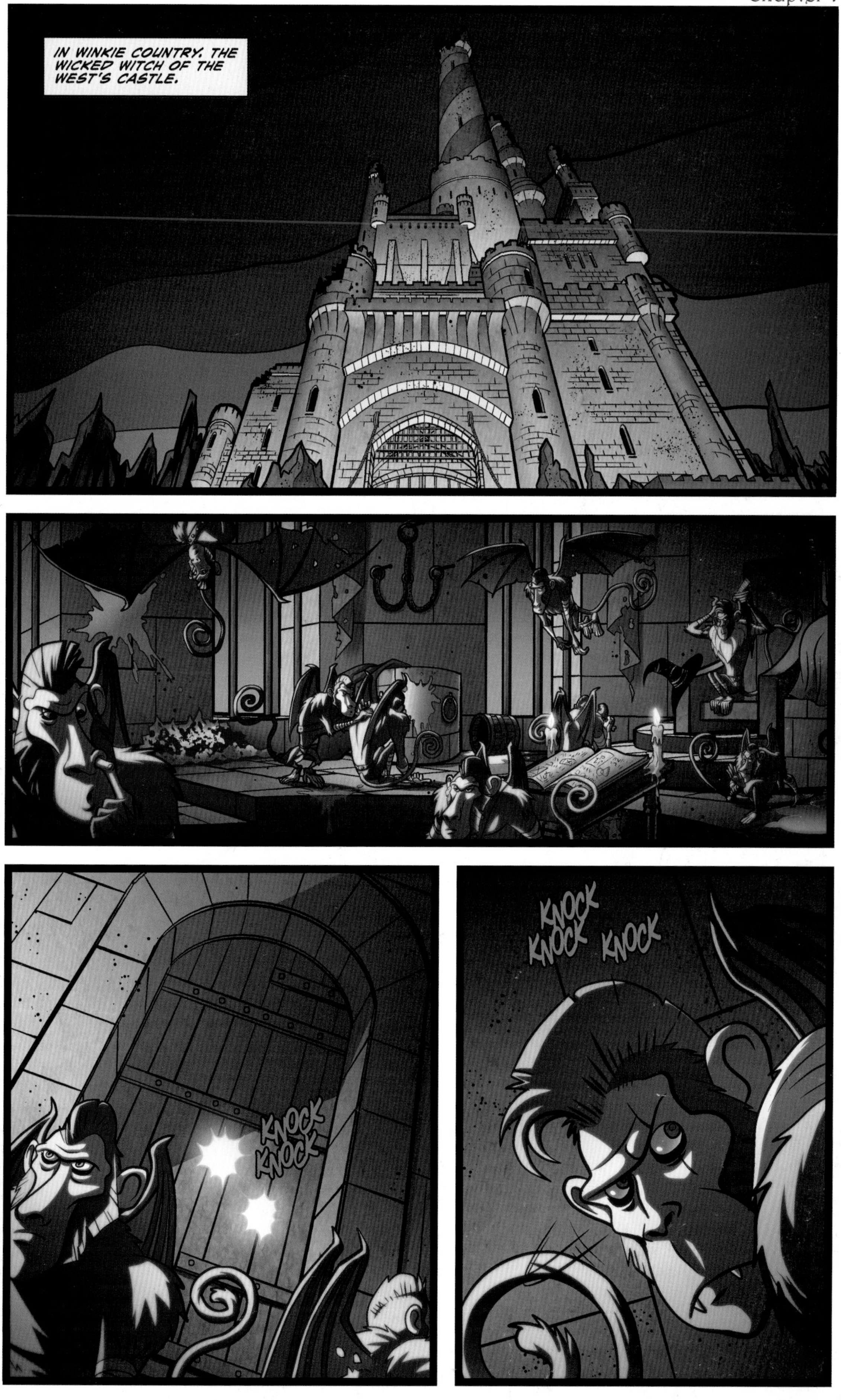
IN WINKIE COUNTRY. THE WICKED WITCH OF THE WEST'S CASTLE.
KNOCK KNOCK
KNOCK KNOCK KNOCK

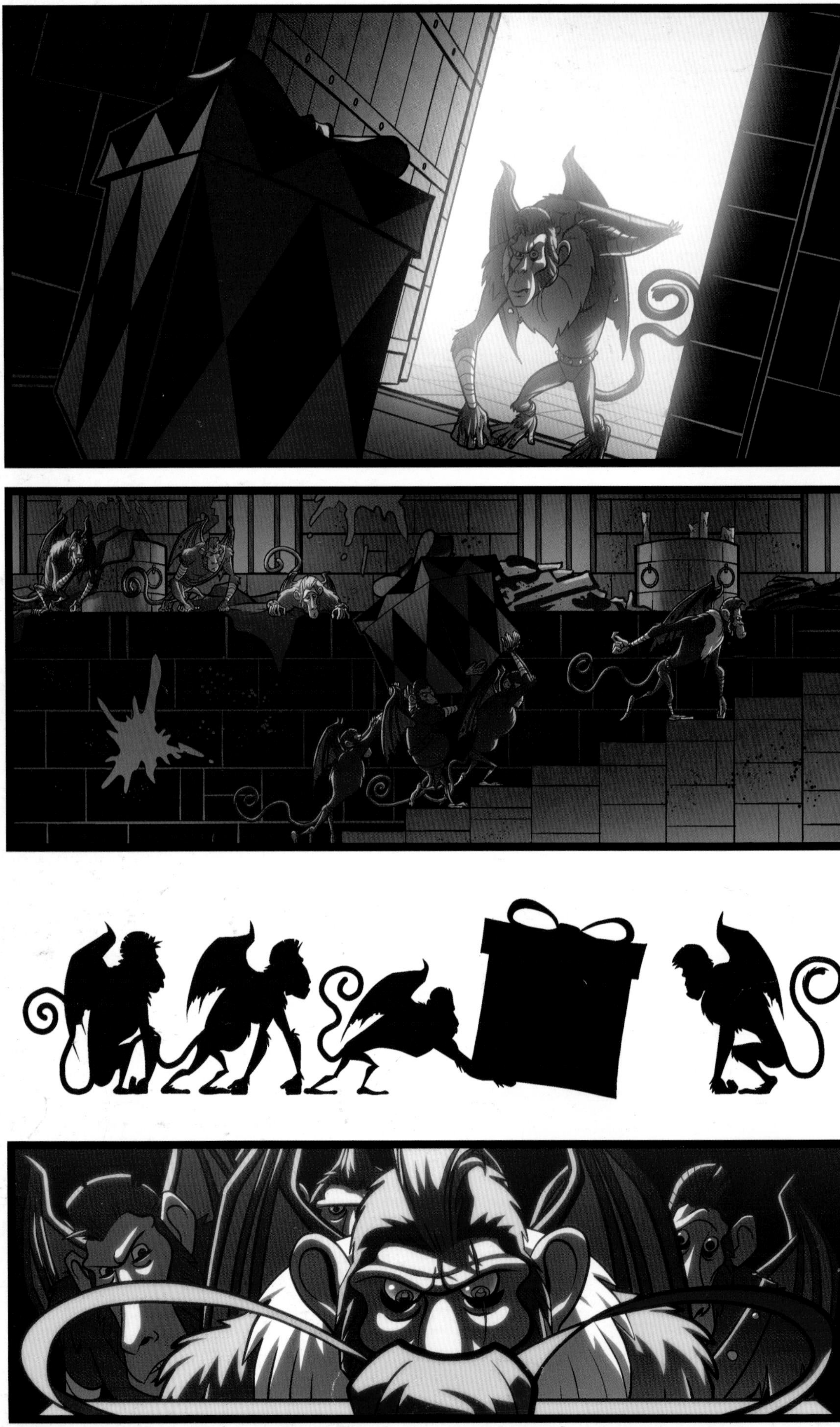

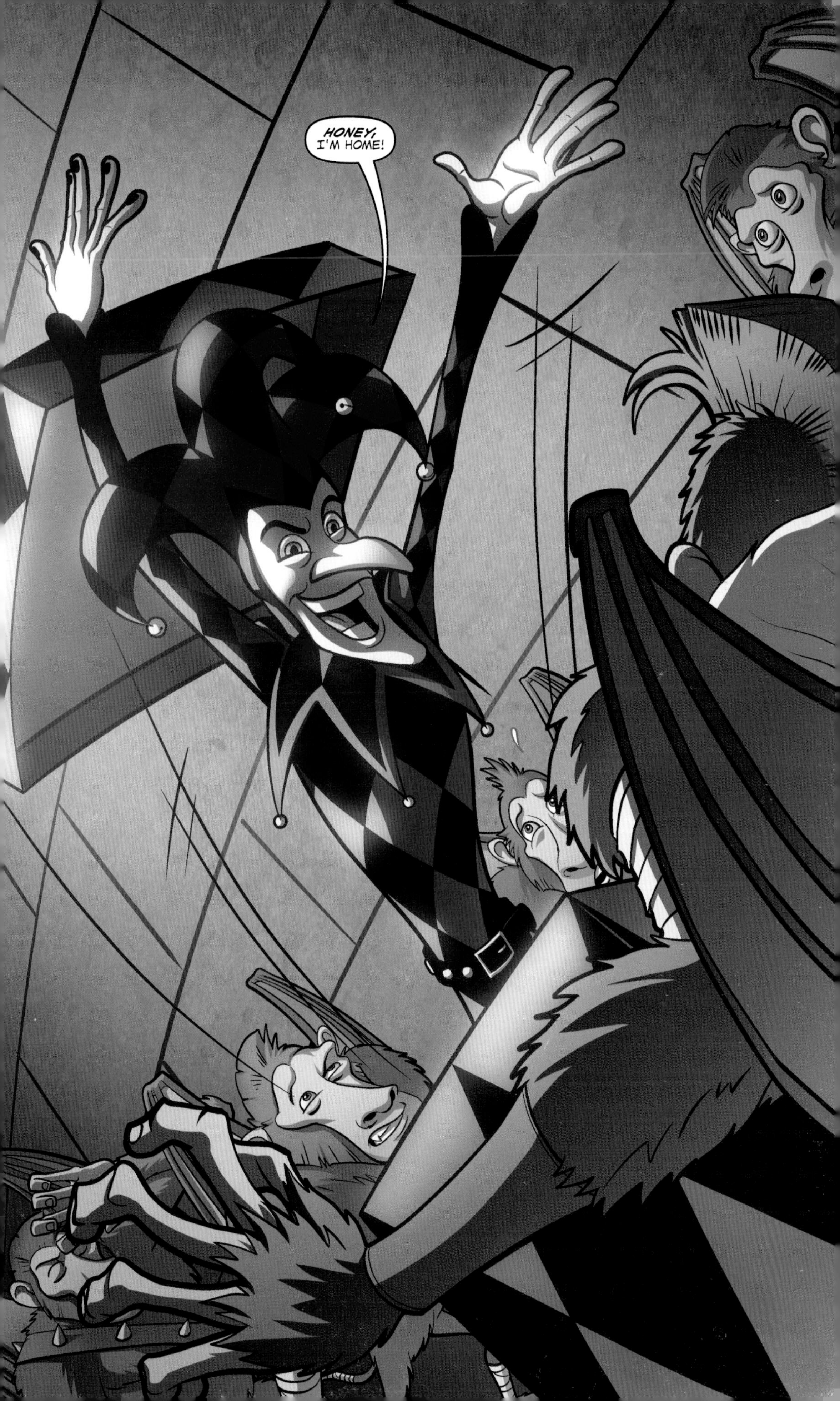
HONEY, I'M HOME!

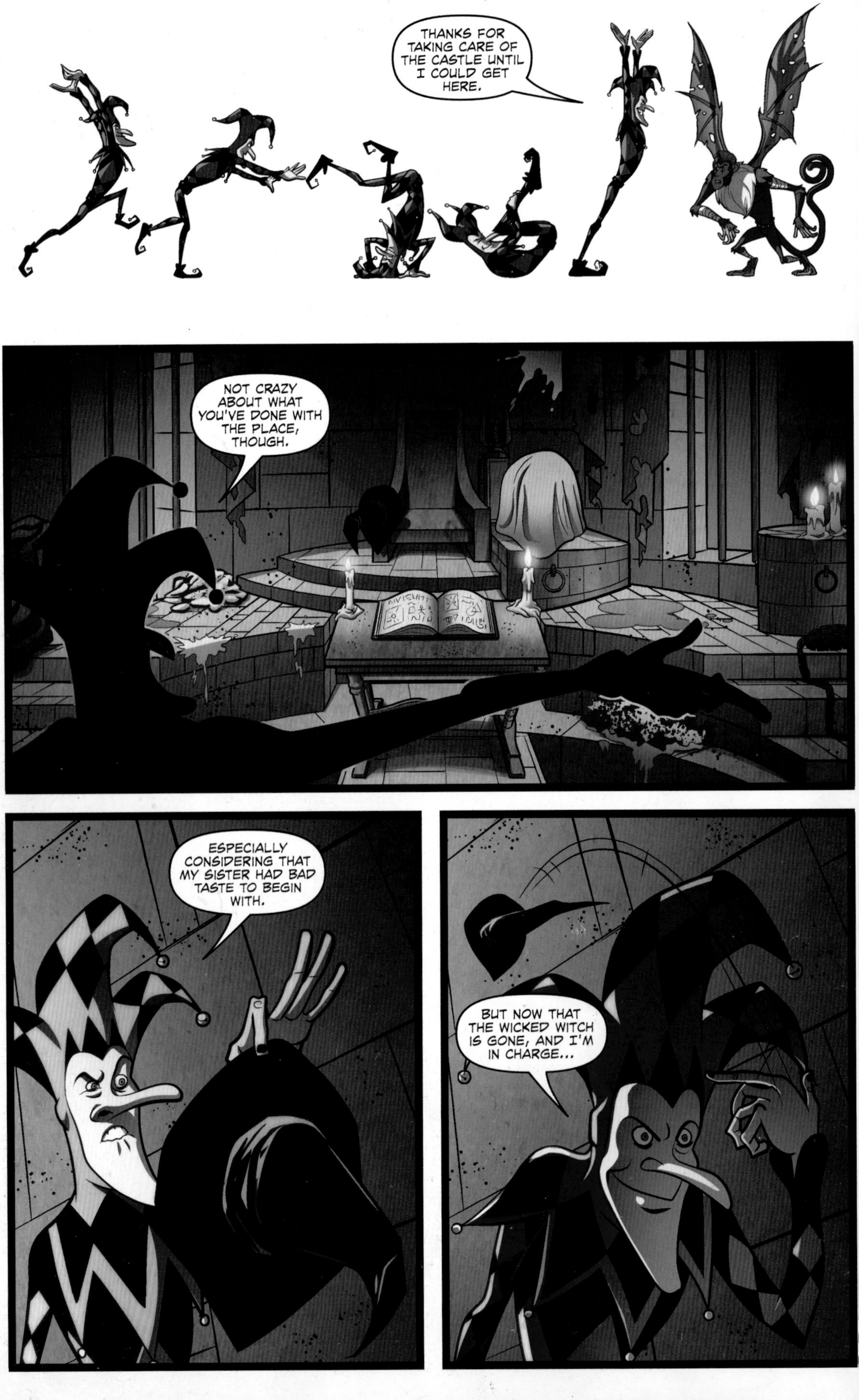
THANKS FOR TAKING CARE OF THE CASTLE UNTIL I COULD GET HERE.
NOT CRAZY ABOUT WHAT YOU'VE DONE WITH THE PLACE, THOUGH.
ESPECIALLY CONSIDERING THAT MY SISTER HAD BAD TASTE TO BEGIN WITH.
BUT NOW THAT THE WICKED WITCH IS GONE, AND I'M IN CHARGE...

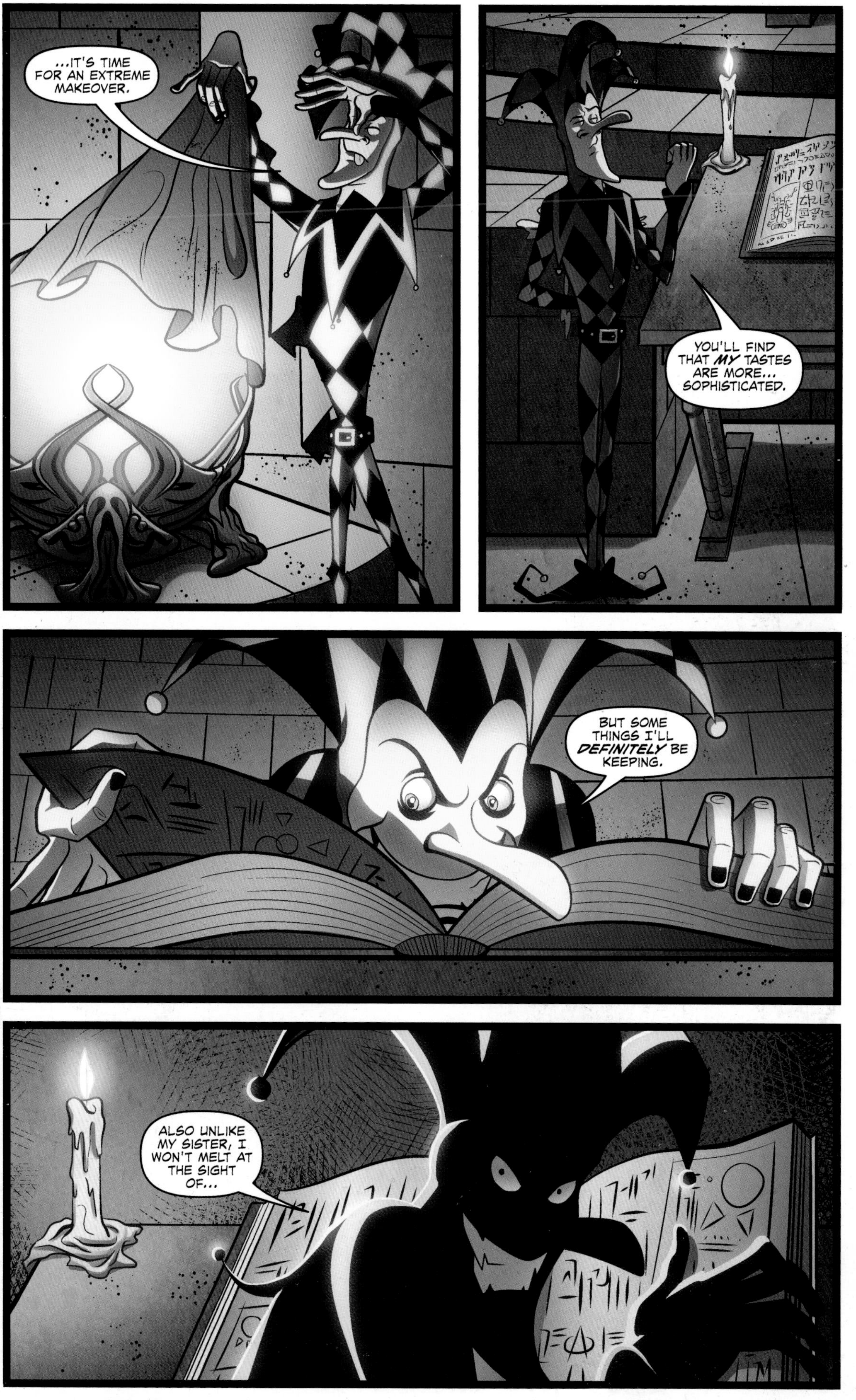
...IT'S TIME FOR AN EXTREME MAKEOVER.
YOU'LL FIND THAT MY TASTES ARE MORE... SOPHISTICATED.
BUT SOME THINGS I'LL DEFINITELY BE KEEPING.
ALSO UNLIKE MY SISTER, I WON'T MELT AT THE SIGHT OF...

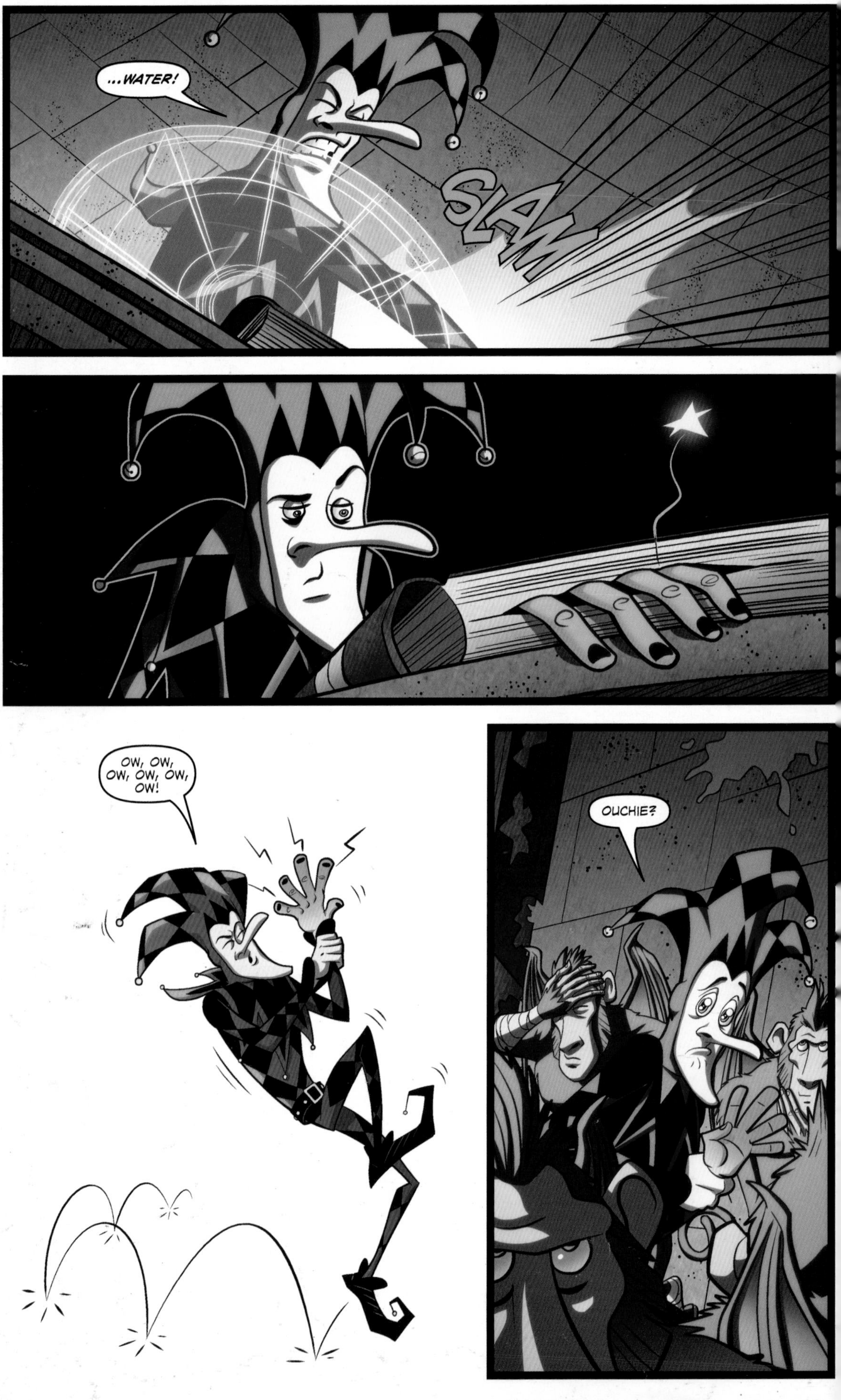
...WATER!
SLAM
OW, OW, OW, OW, OW, OW!
OUCHIE?

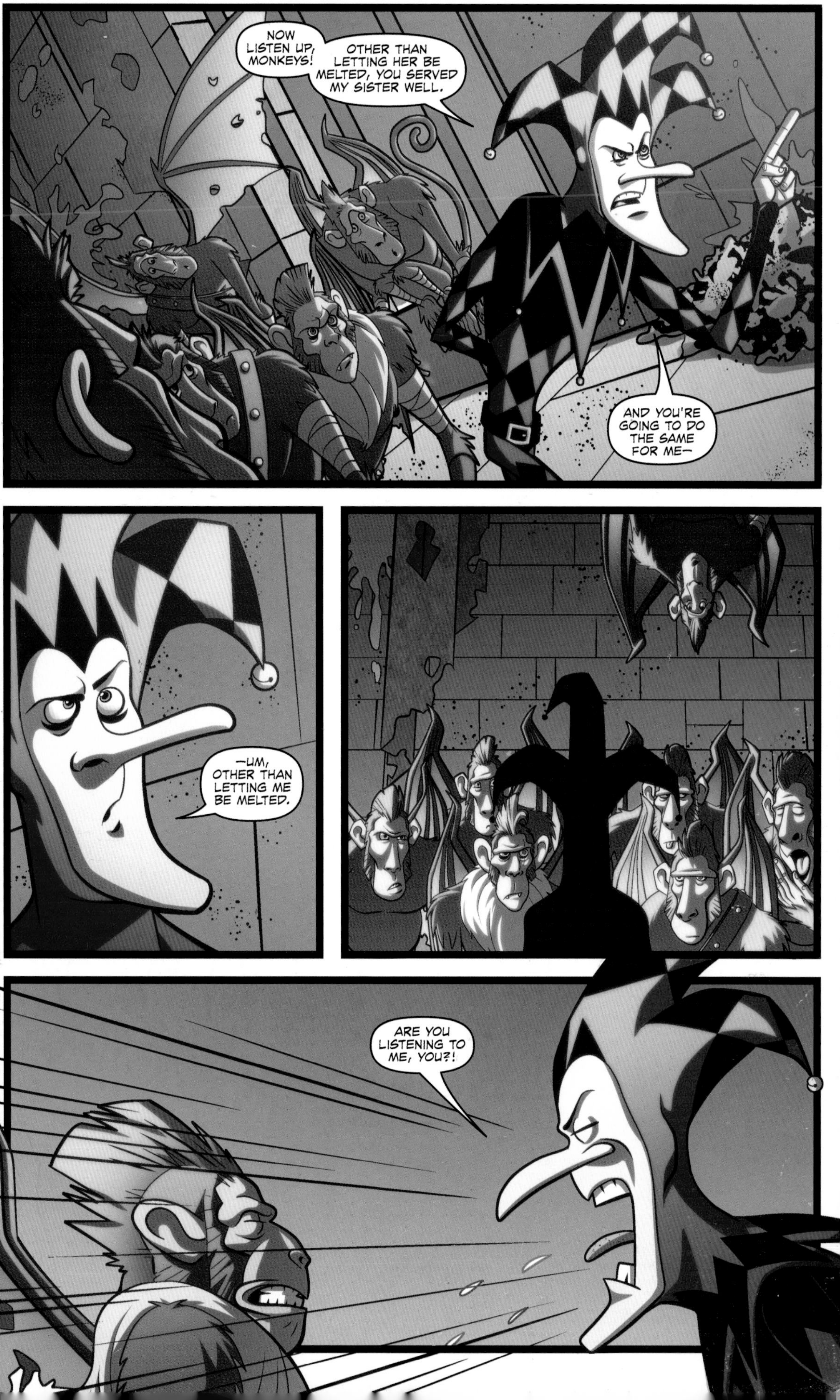
NOW LISTEN UP, MONKEYS!
OTHER THAN LETTING HER BE MELTED, YOU SERVED MY SISTER WELL.
AND YOU'RE GOING TO DO THE SAME FOR ME—
—UM, OTHER THAN LETTING ME BE MELTED.
ARE YOU LISTENING TO ME, YOU?!

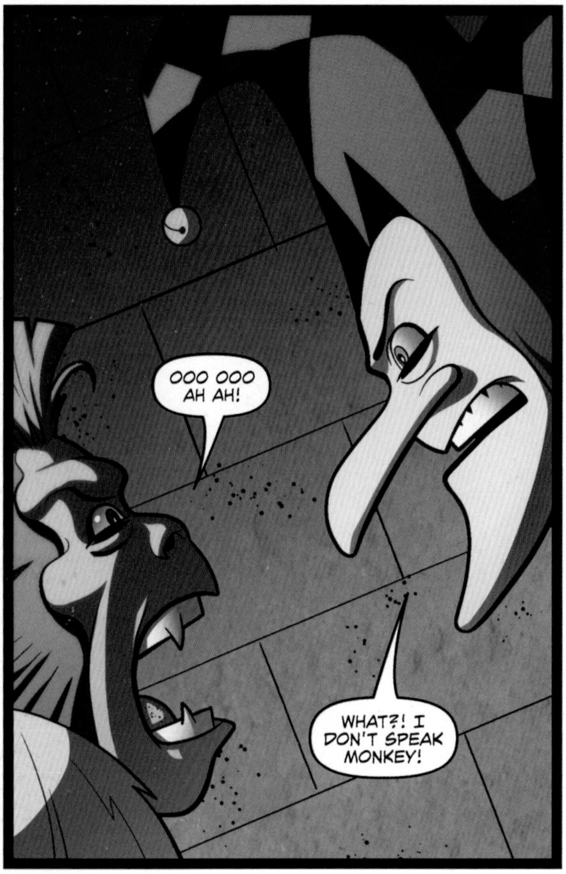
OOO OOO
AH AH!
WHAT?! I DON'T SPEAK MONKEY!

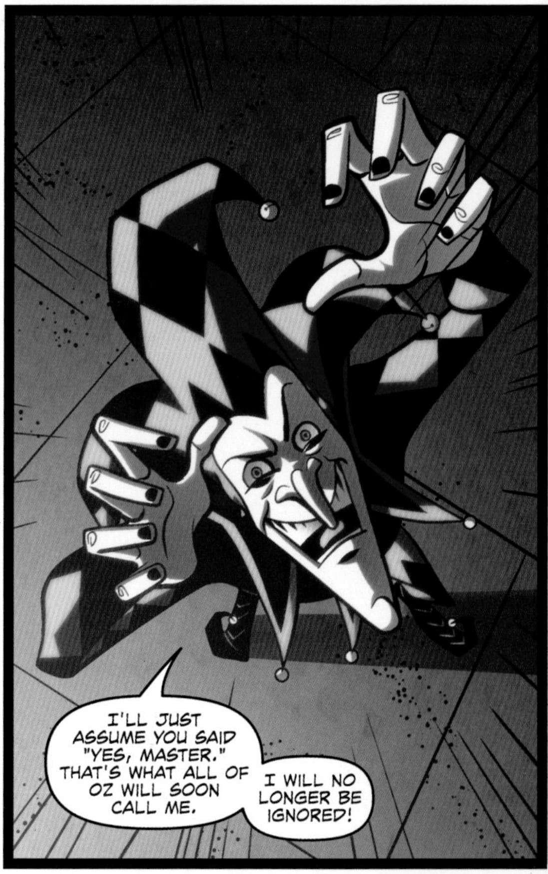
I'LL JUST ASSUME YOU SAID "YES, MASTER." THAT'S WHAT ALL OF OZ WILL SOON CALL ME.
I WILL NO LONGER BE IGNORED!

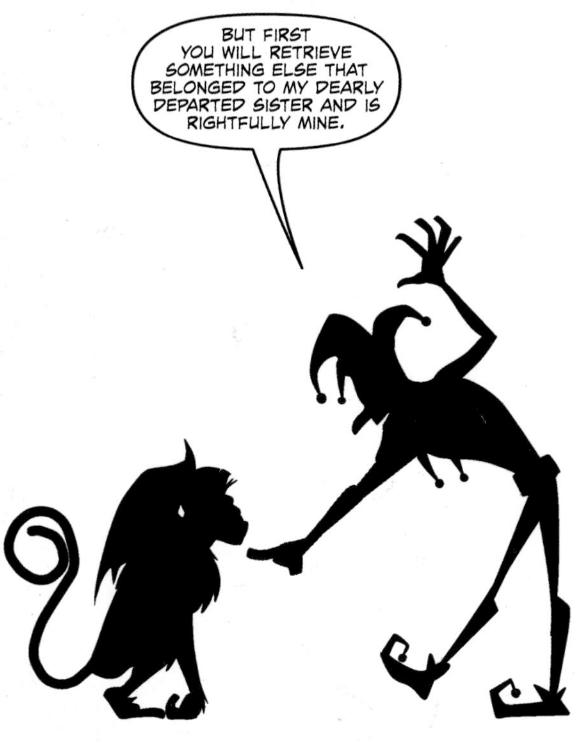
BUT FIRST YOU WILL RETRIEVE SOMETHING ELSE THAT BELONGED TO MY DEARLY DEPARTED SISTER AND IS RIGHTFULLY MINE.

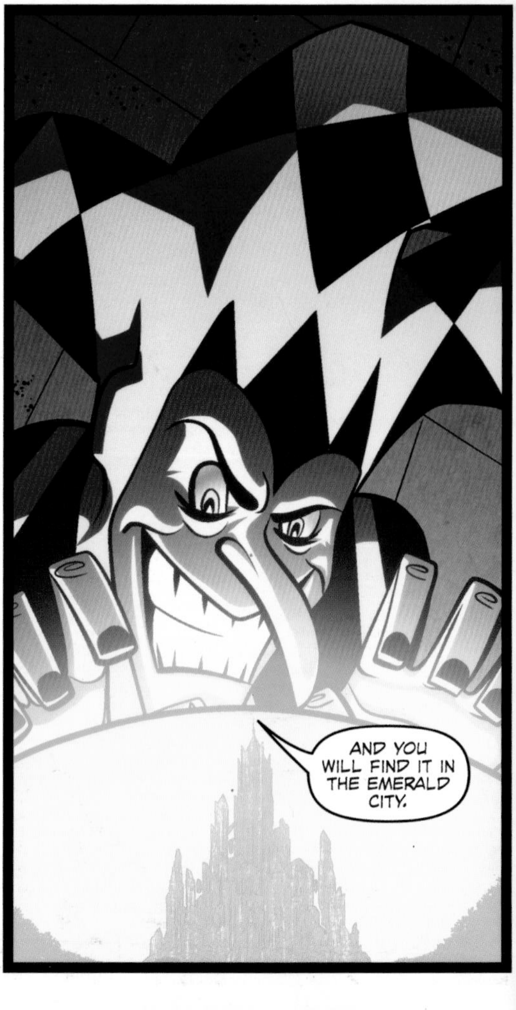
AND YOU WILL FIND IT IN THE EMERALD CITY.

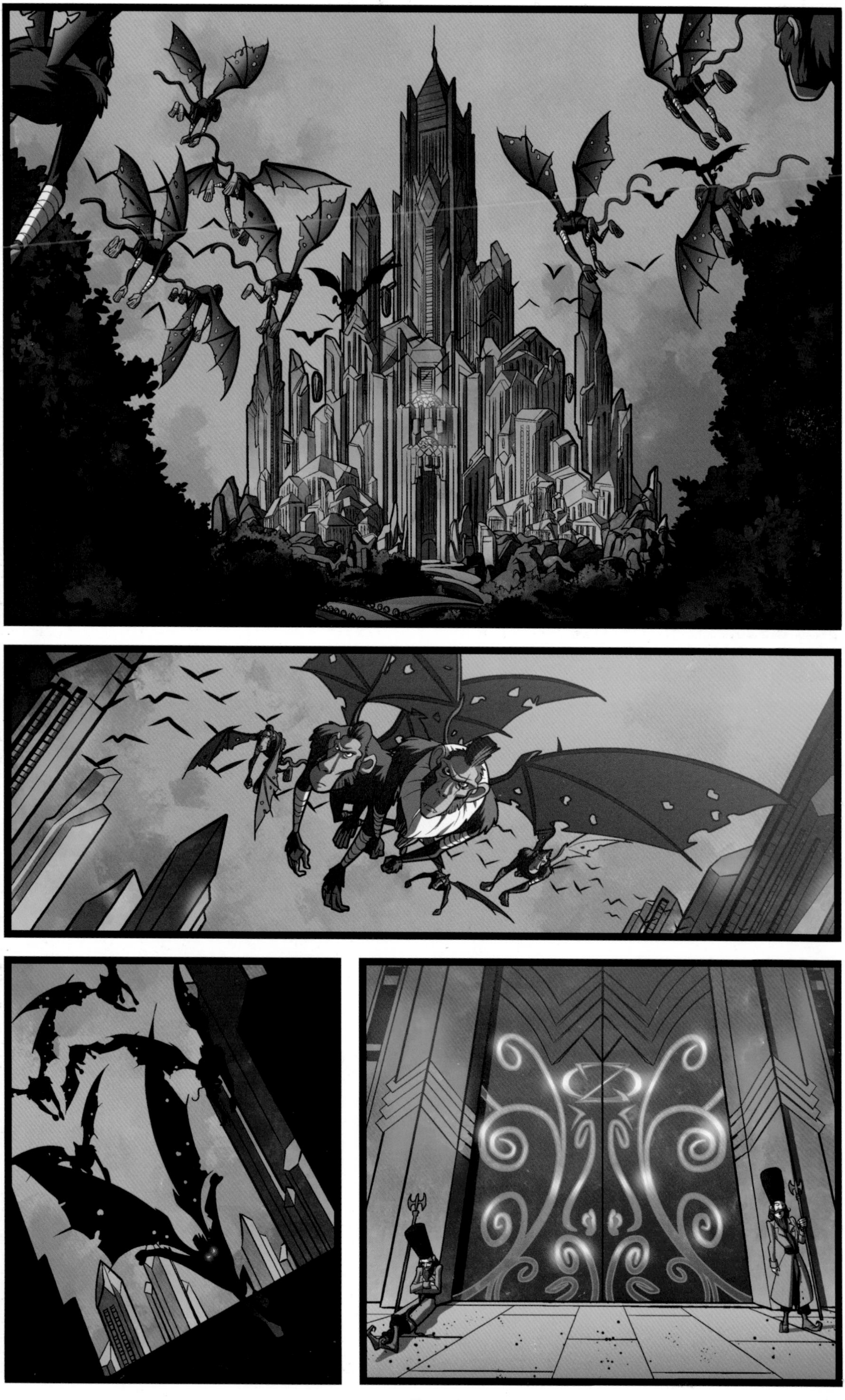

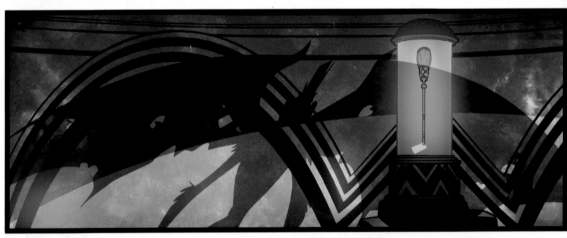

"THE WICKED WITCH'S BROOMSTICK HAS BEEN STOLEN?"

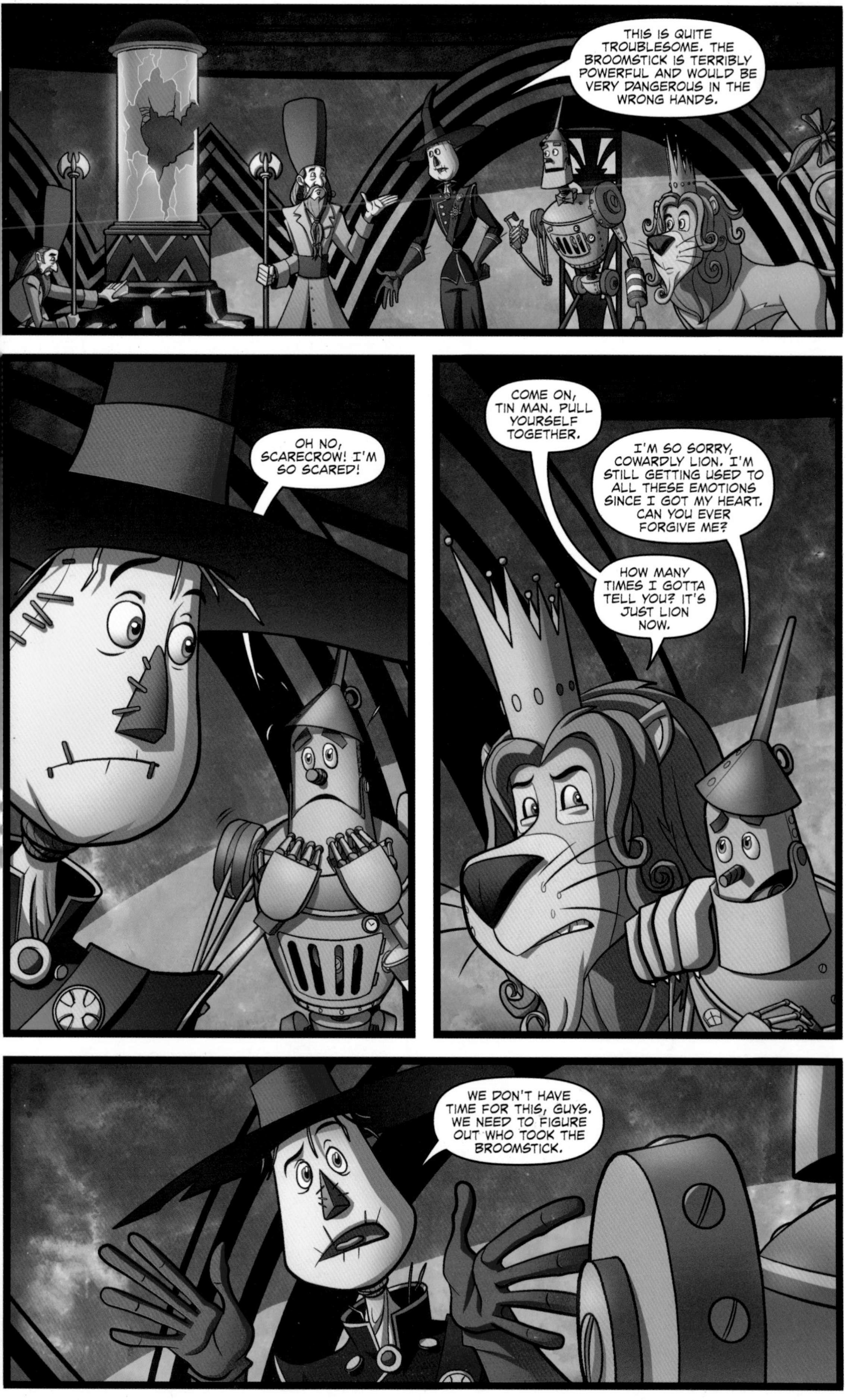

THIS IS QUITE TROUBLESOME. THE BROOMSTICK IS TERRIBLY POWERFUL AND WOULD BE VERY DANGEROUS IN THE WRONG HANDS.
OH NO, SCARECROW! I'M SO SCARED!
COME ON, TIN MAN. PULL YOURSELF TOGETHER.
I'M SO SORRY, COWARDLY LION. I'M STILL GETTING USED TO ALL THESE EMOTIONS SINCE I GOT MY HEART. CAN YOU EVER FORGIVE ME?
HOW MANY TIMES I GOTTA TELL YOU? IT'S JUST LION NOW.
WE DON'T HAVE TIME FOR THIS, GUYS. WE NEED TO FIGURE OUT WHO TOOK THE BROOMSTICK.

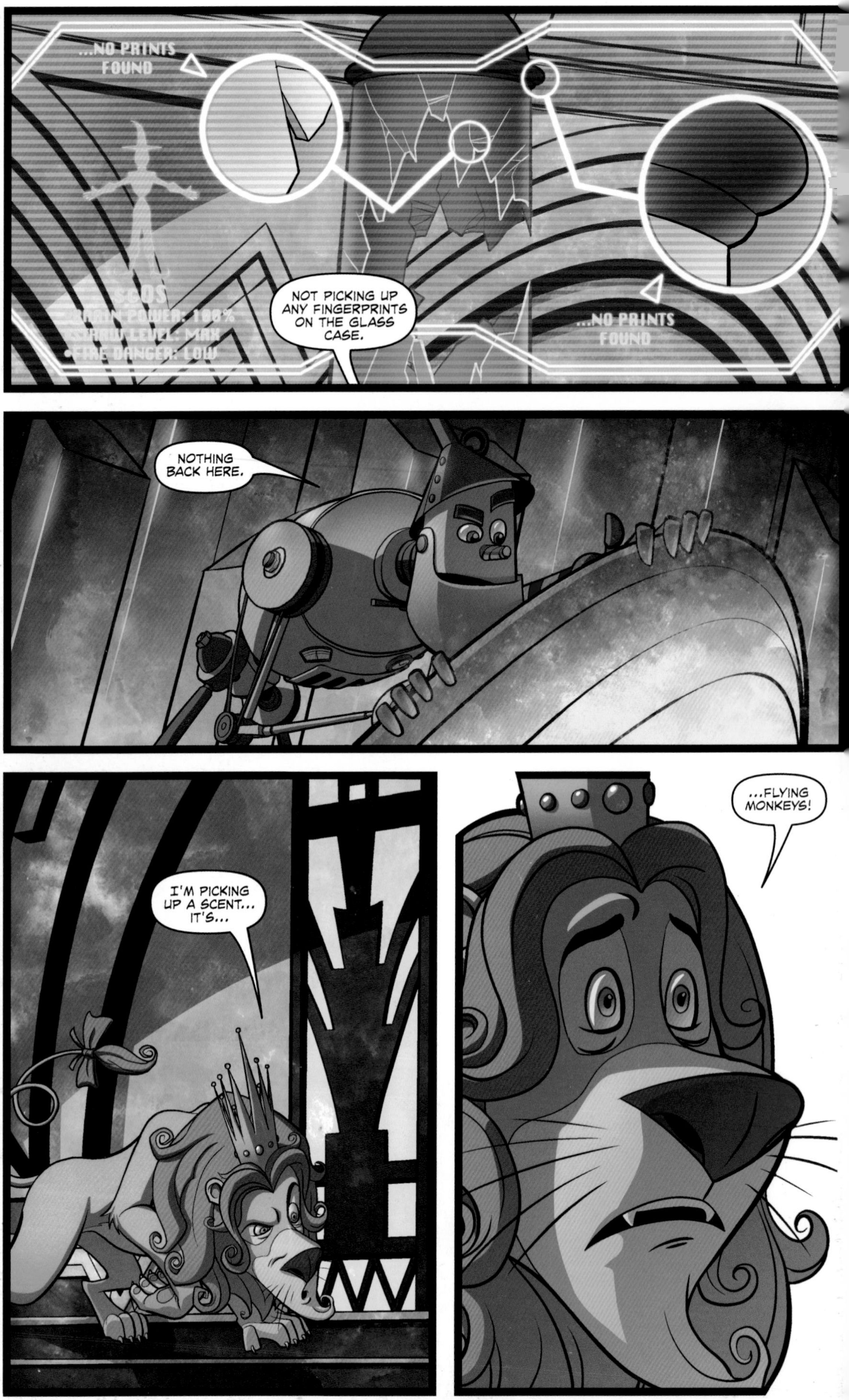
...NO PRINTS FOUND
SCOS
•FIRE DANGER: LOW
NOT PICKING UP ANY FINGERPRINTS ON THE GLASS CASE.
...NO PRINTS FOUND
NOTHING BACK HERE.
I'M PICKING UP A SCENT... IT'S...
...FLYING MONKEYS!

NOW I'M REALLY SCARED!

I'M NOT SCARED OF A LITTLE MONKEY WITH WINGS!

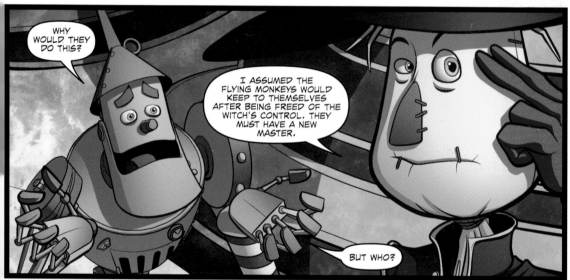

WHY WOULD THEY DO THIS?

I ASSUMED THE FLYING MONKEYS WOULD KEEP TO THEMSELVES AFTER BEING FREED OF THE WITCH'S CONTROL. THEY MUST HAVE A NEW MASTER.

BUT WHO?

I SUSPECT WE'LL FIND OUT SOON ENOUGH.

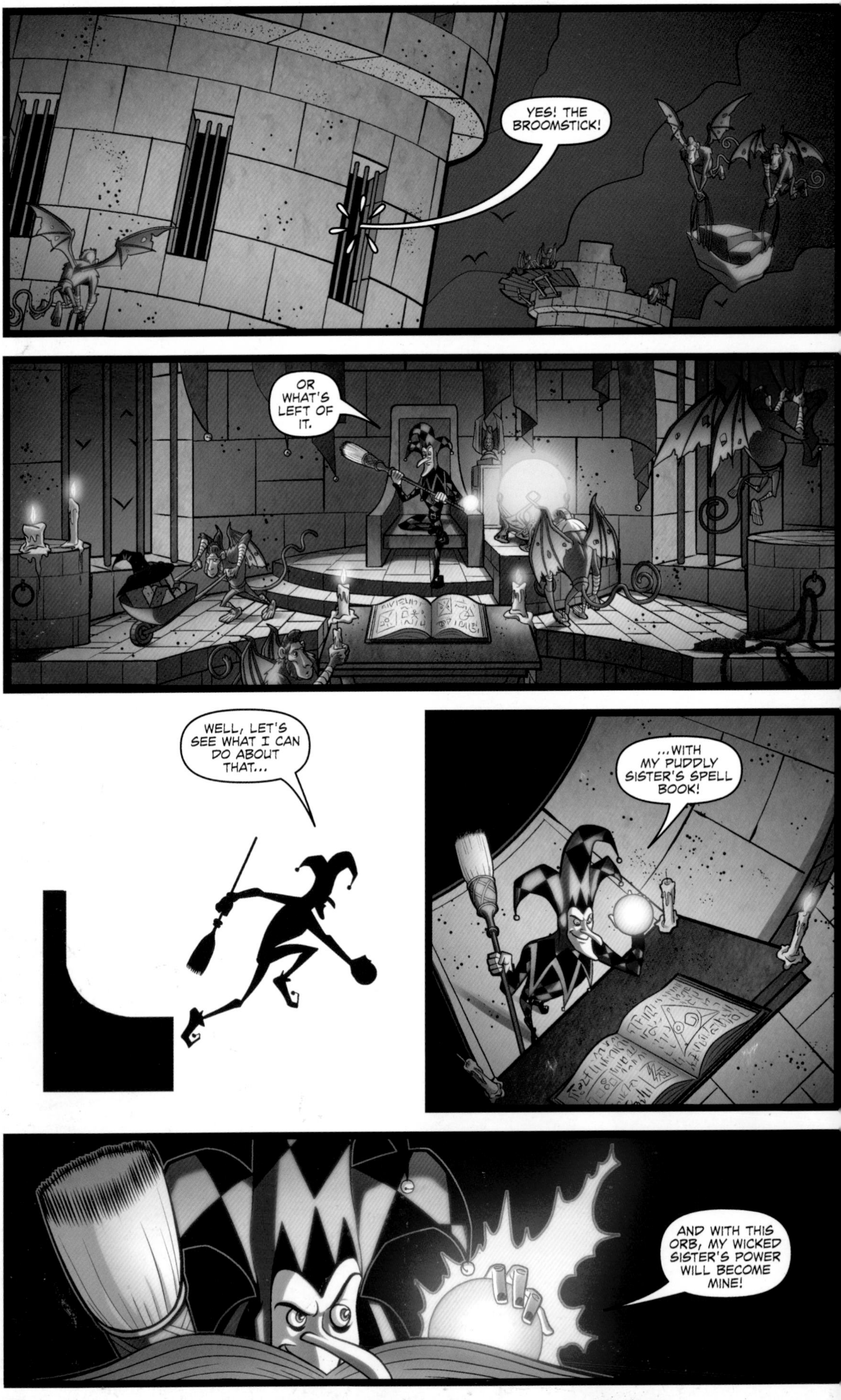
YES! THE BROOMSTICK!
OR WHAT'S LEFT OF IT.
WELL, LET'S SEE WHAT I CAN DO ABOUT THAT...
...WITH MY PUDDLY SISTER'S SPELL BOOK!
AND WITH THIS ORB, MY WICKED SISTER'S POWER WILL BECOME MINE!

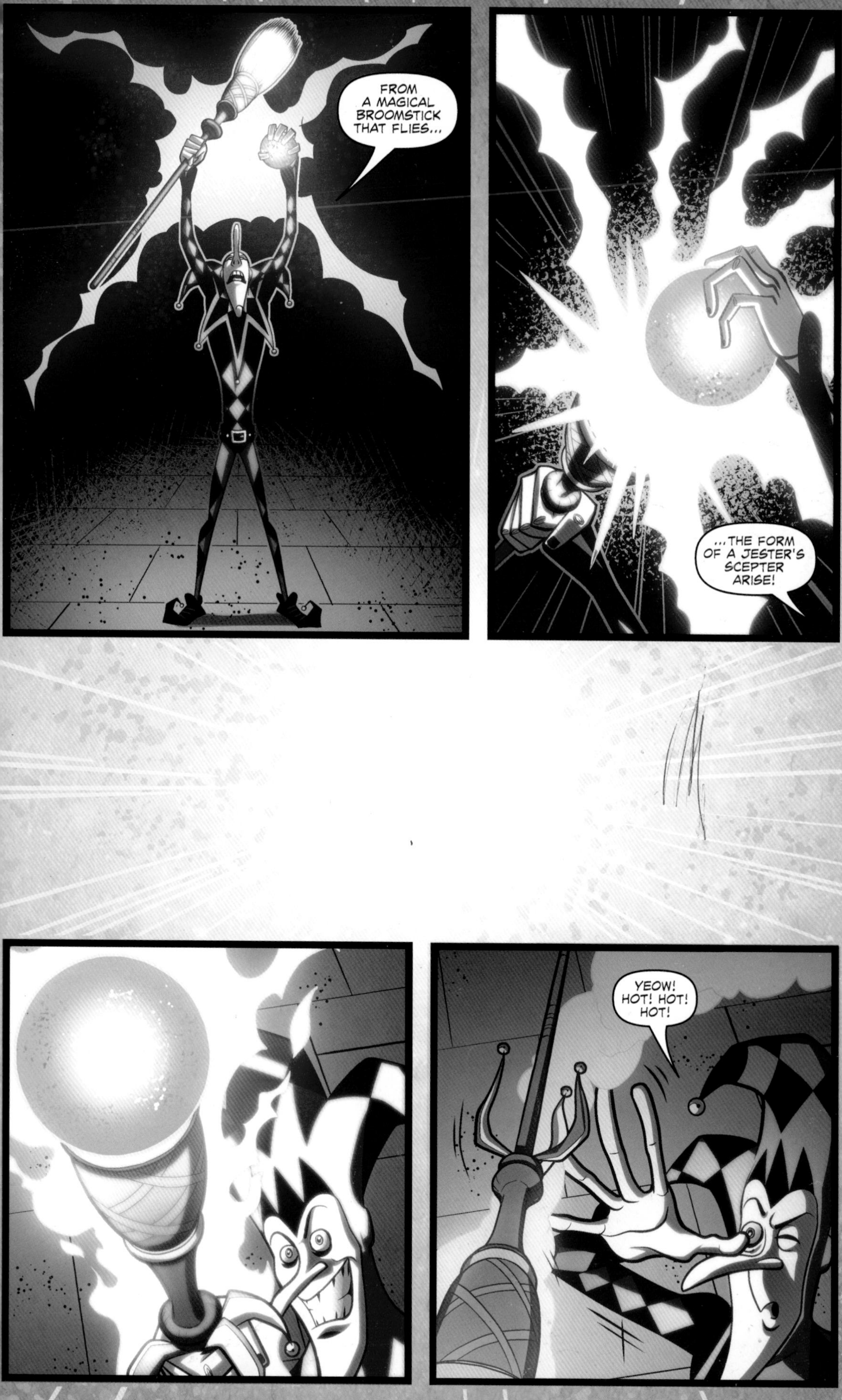
FROM A MAGICAL BROOMSTICK THAT FLIES...
...THE FORM OF A JESTER'S SCEPTER ARISE!
YEOW! HOT! HOT! HOT!

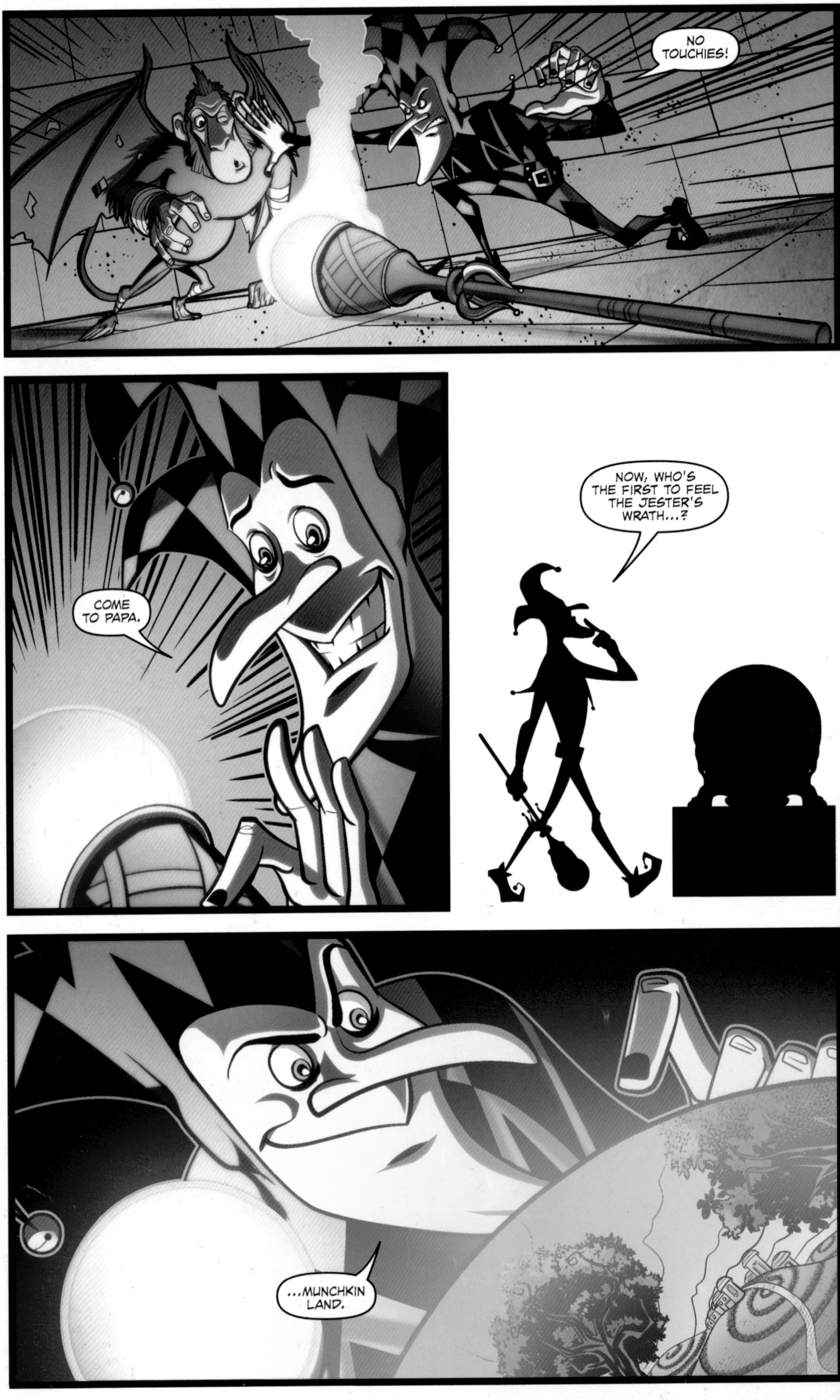
NO TOUCHIES!
COME TO PAPA.
NOW, WHO'S THE FIRST TO FEEL THE JESTER'S WRATH...?
...MUNCHKIN LAND.

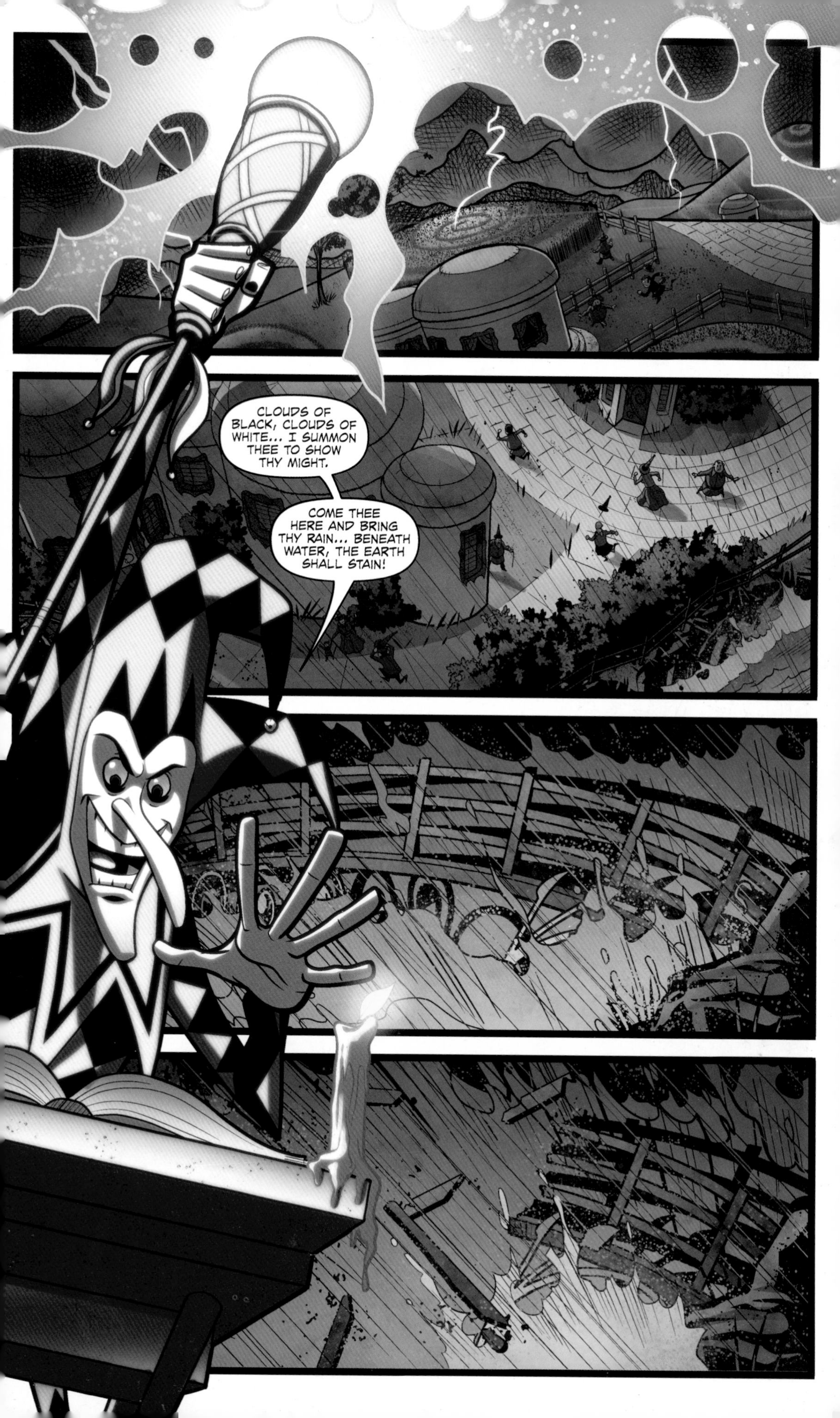
CLOUDS OF BLACK, CLOUDS OF WHITE... I SUMMON THEE TO SHOW THY MIGHT.
COME THEE HERE AND BRING THY RAIN... BENEATH WATER, THE EARTH SHALL STAIN!

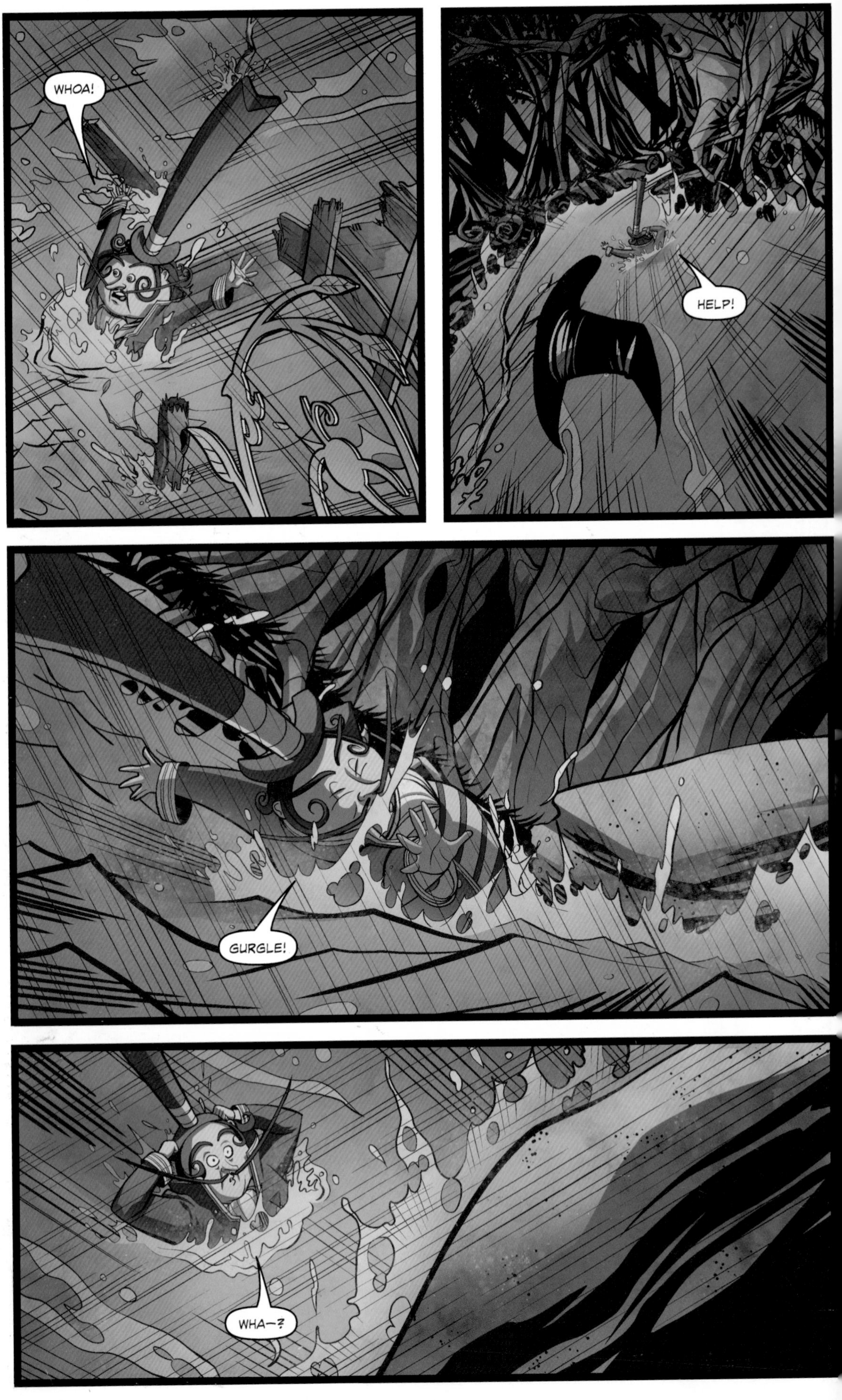
WHOA!
HELP!
GURGLE!
WHA—?

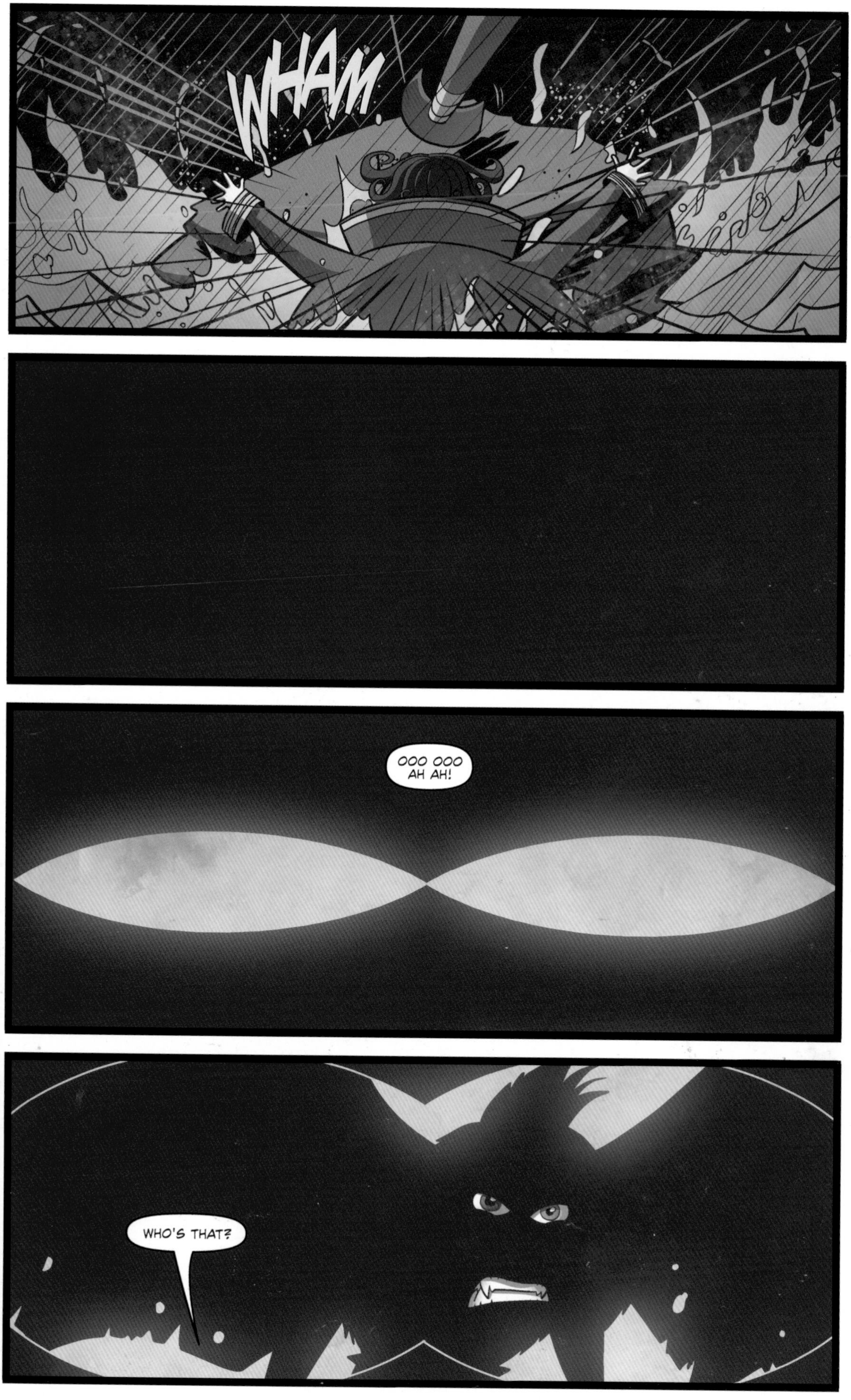
WHAM
OOO OOO AH AH!
WHO'S THAT?

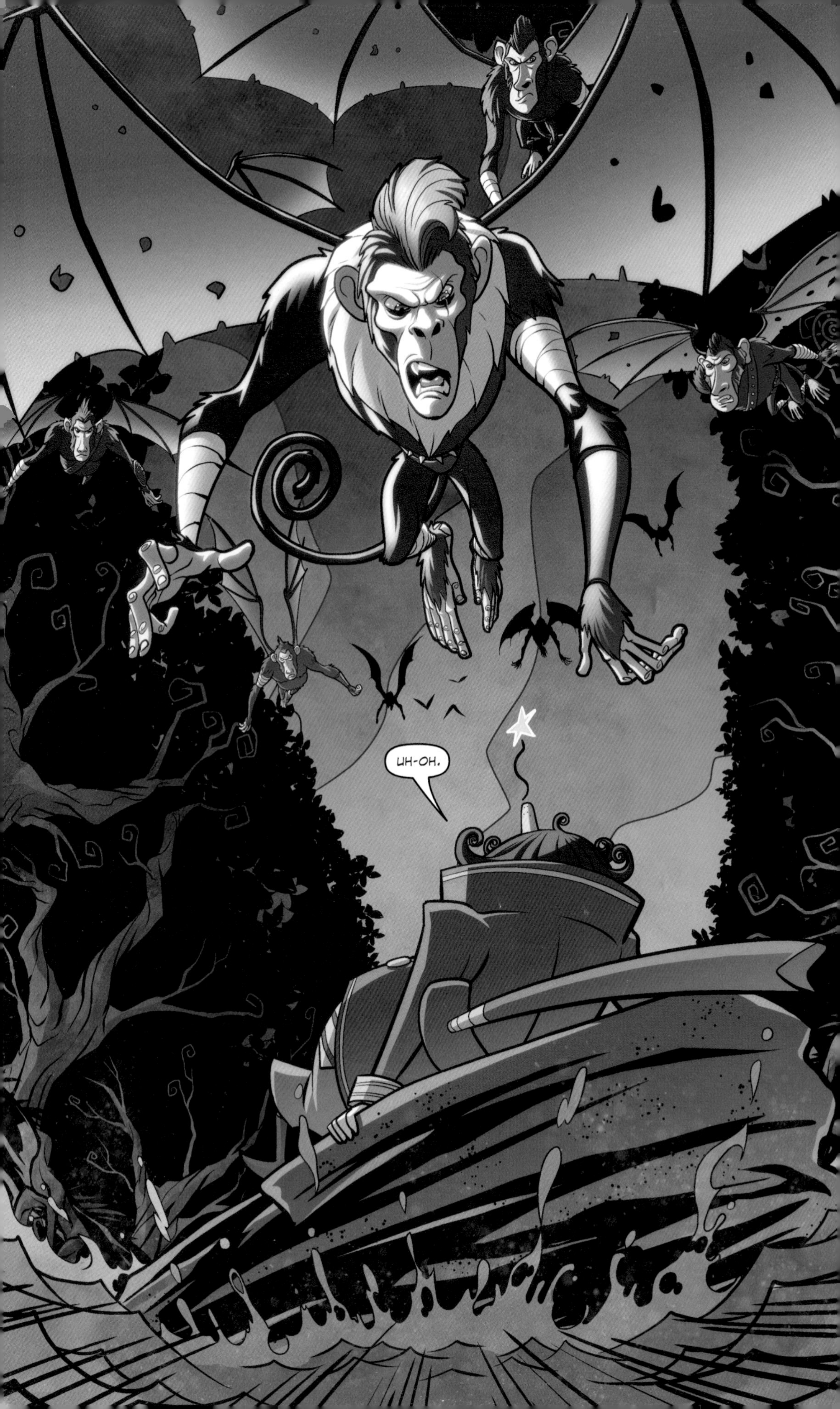
UH-OH.

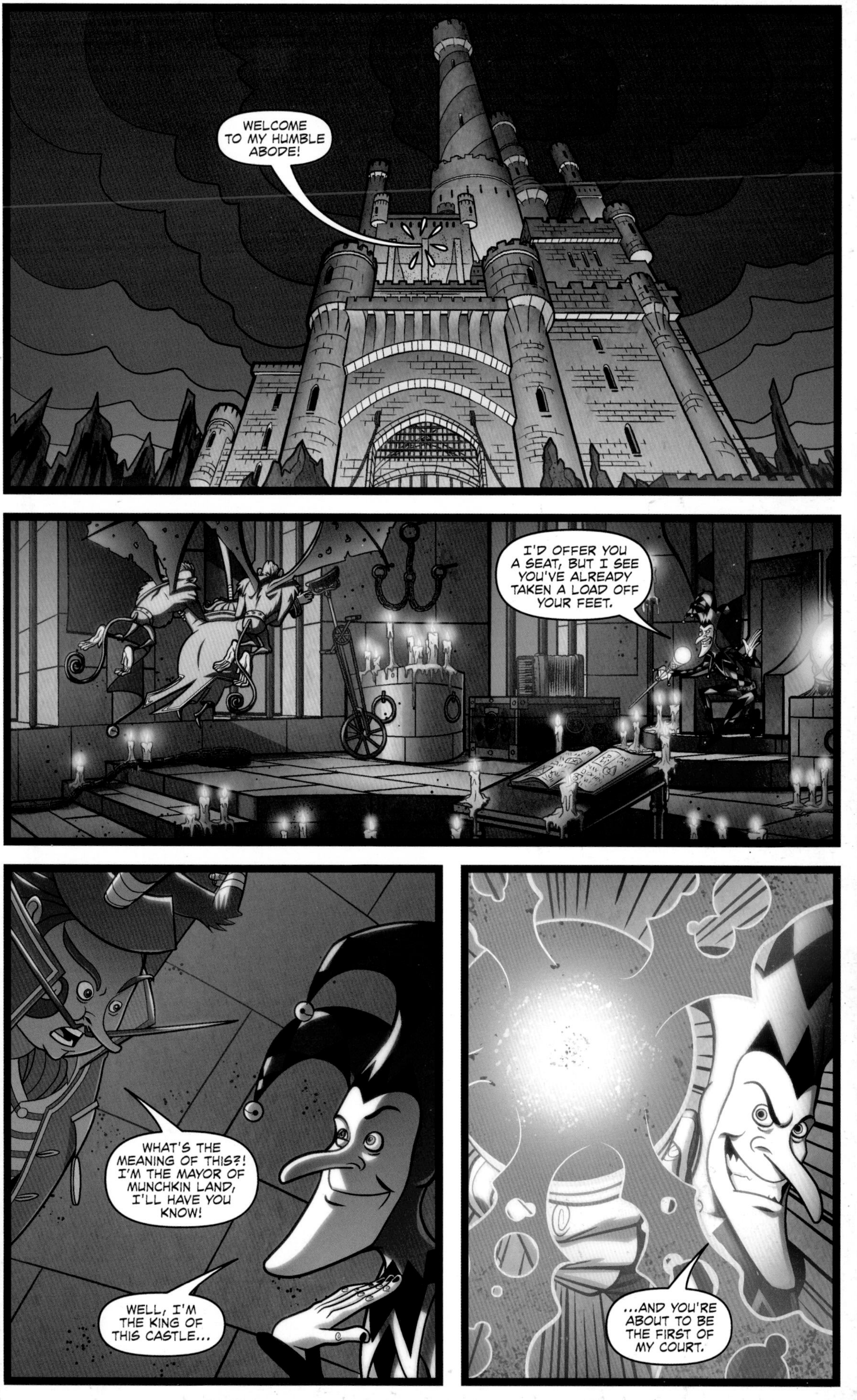
WELCOME TO MY HUMBLE ABODE!
I'D OFFER YOU A SEAT, BUT I SEE YOU'VE ALREADY TAKEN A LOAD OFF YOUR FEET.
WHAT'S THE MEANING OF THIS?! I'M THE MAYOR OF MUNCHKIN LAND, I'LL HAVE YOU KNOW!
WELL, I'M THE KING OF THIS CASTLE...
...AND YOU'RE ABOUT TO BE THE FIRST OF MY COURT.

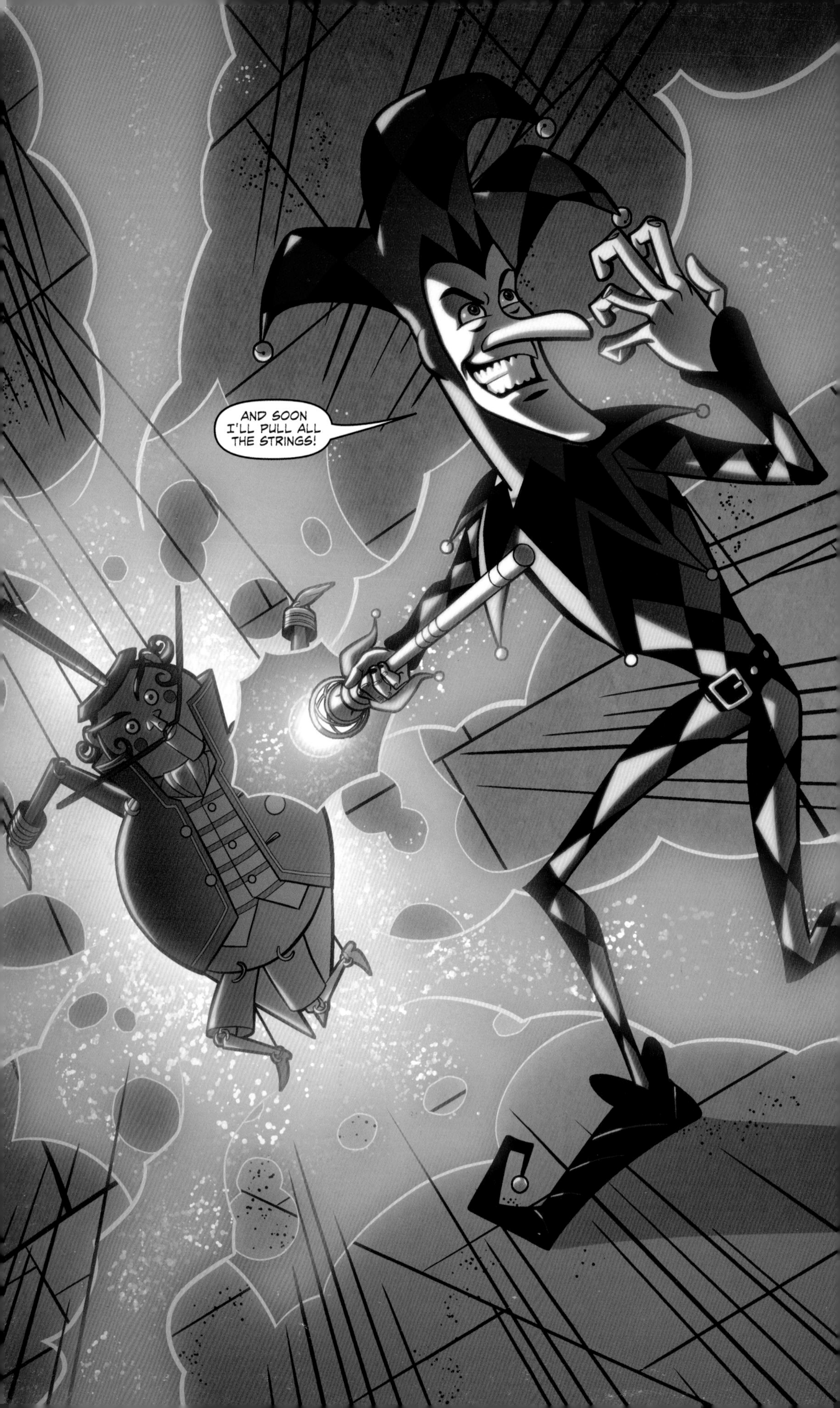
AND SOON I'LL PULL ALL THE STRINGS!

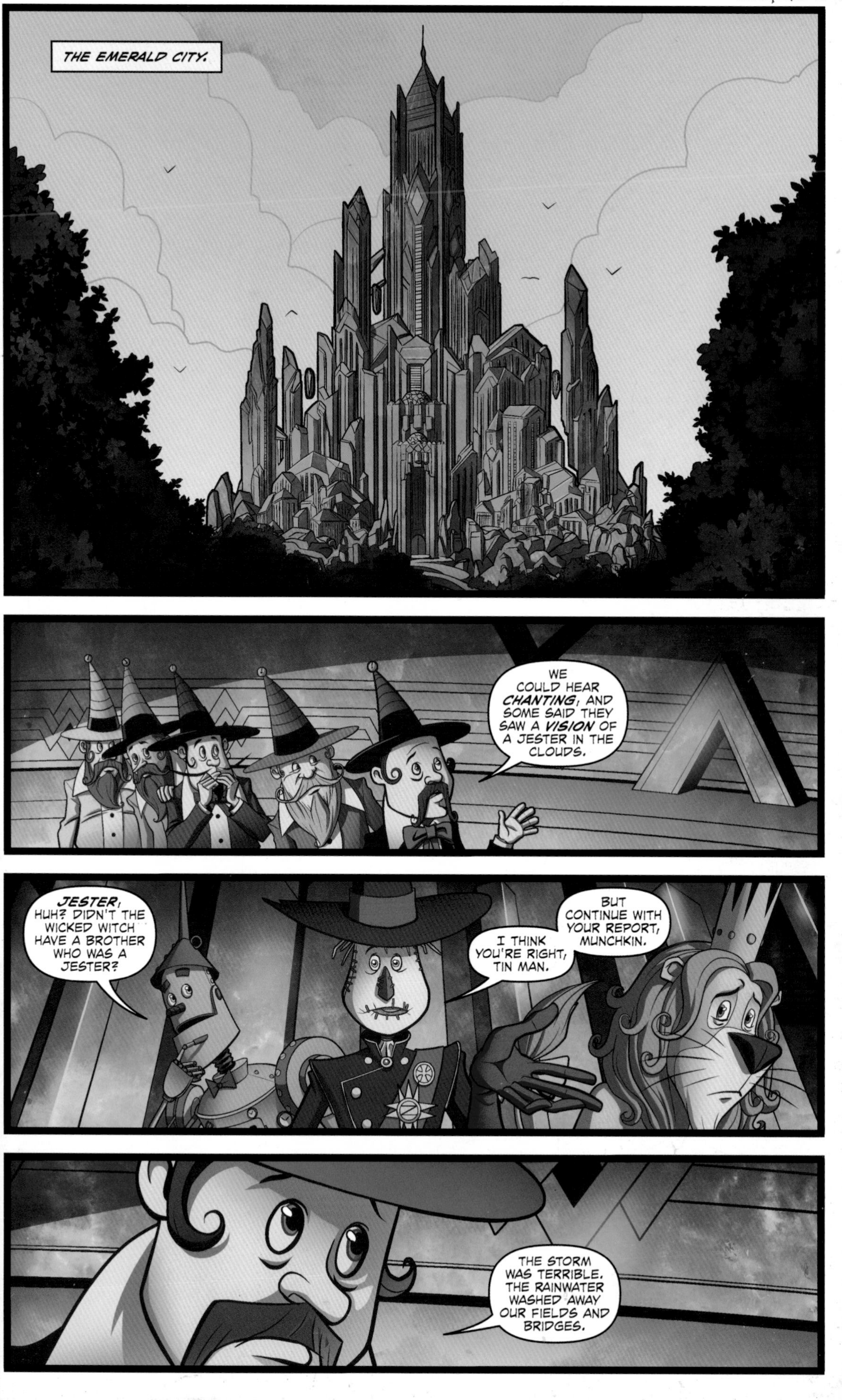
THE EMERALD CITY.
WE COULD HEAR CHANTING, AND SOME SAID THEY SAW A VISION OF A JESTER IN THE CLOUDS.
JESTER, HUH? DIDN'T THE WICKED WITCH HAVE A BROTHER WHO WAS A JESTER?
I THINK YOU'RE RIGHT, TIN MAN.
BUT CONTINUE WITH YOUR REPORT, MUNCHKIN.
THE STORM WAS TERRIBLE. THE RAINWATER WASHED AWAY OUR FIELDS AND BRIDGES.

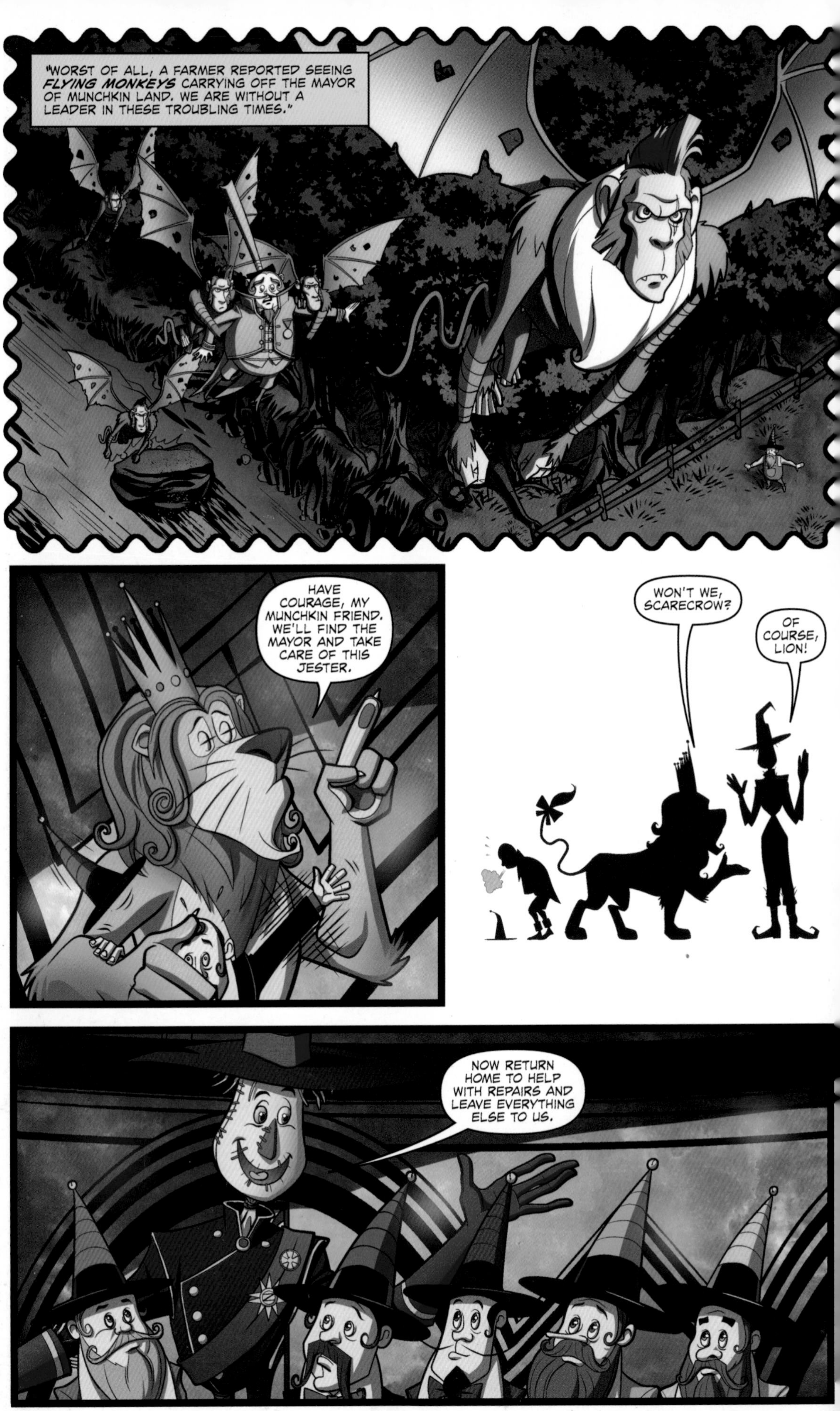
"WORST OF ALL, A FARMER REPORTED SEEING FLYING MONKEYS CARRYING OFF THE MAYOR OF MUNCHKIN LAND. WE ARE WITHOUT A LEADER IN THESE TROUBLING TIMES."
HAVE COURAGE, MY MUNCHKIN FRIEND. WE'LL FIND THE MAYOR AND TAKE CARE OF THIS JESTER.
WON'T WE, SCARECROW?
OF COURSE, LION!
NOW RETURN HOME TO HELP WITH REPAIRS AND LEAVE EVERYTHING ELSE TO US.

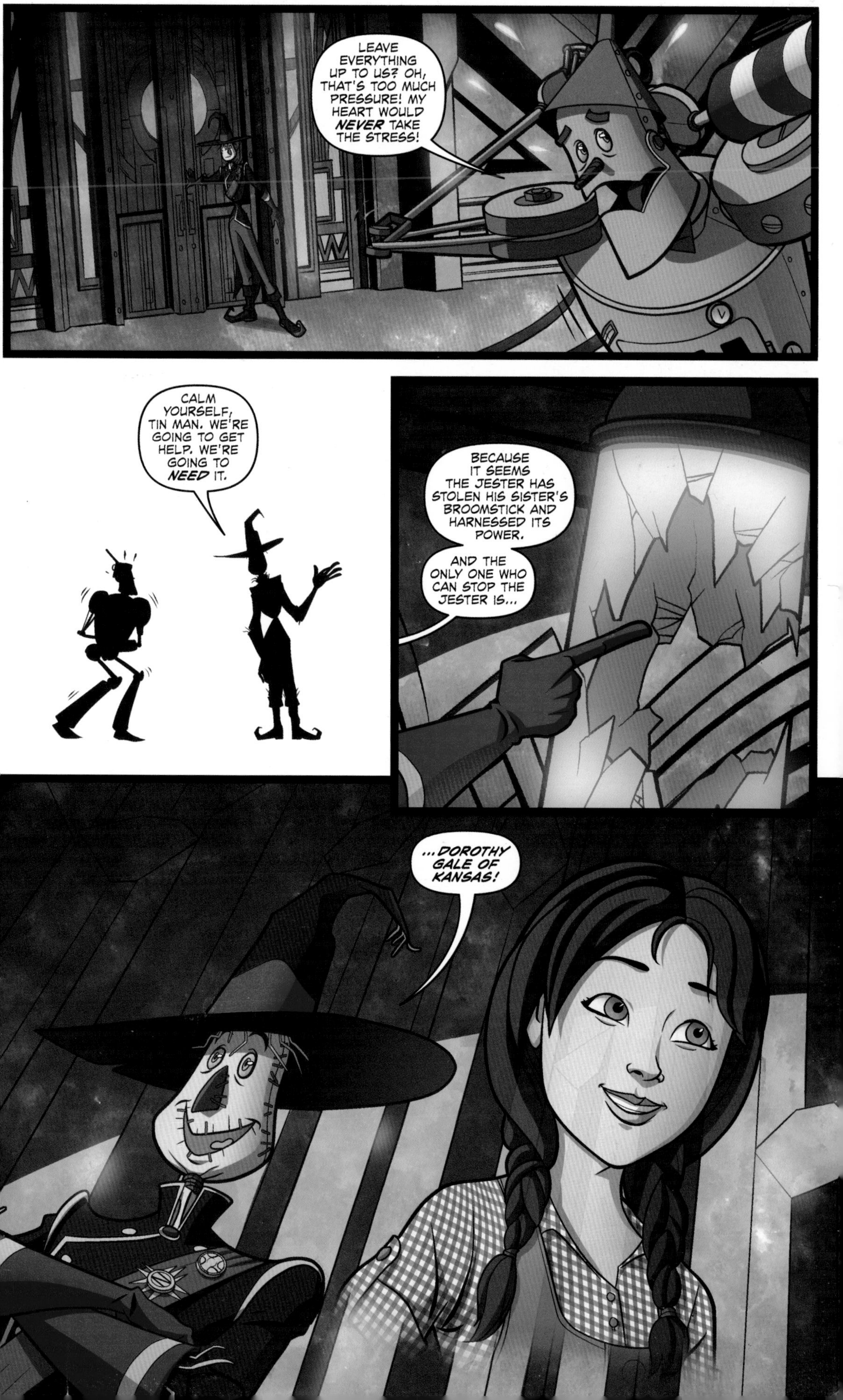
LEAVE EVERYTHING UP TO US? OH, THAT'S TOO MUCH PRESSURE! MY HEART WOULD NEVER TAKE THE STRESS!
CALM YOURSELF, TIN MAN. WE'RE GOING TO GET HELP. WE'RE GOING TO NEED IT.
BECAUSE IT SEEMS THE JESTER HAS STOLEN HIS SISTER'S BROOMSTICK AND HARNESSED ITS POWER.
AND THE ONLY ONE WHO CAN STOP THE JESTER IS...
...DOROTHY GALE OF KANSAS!

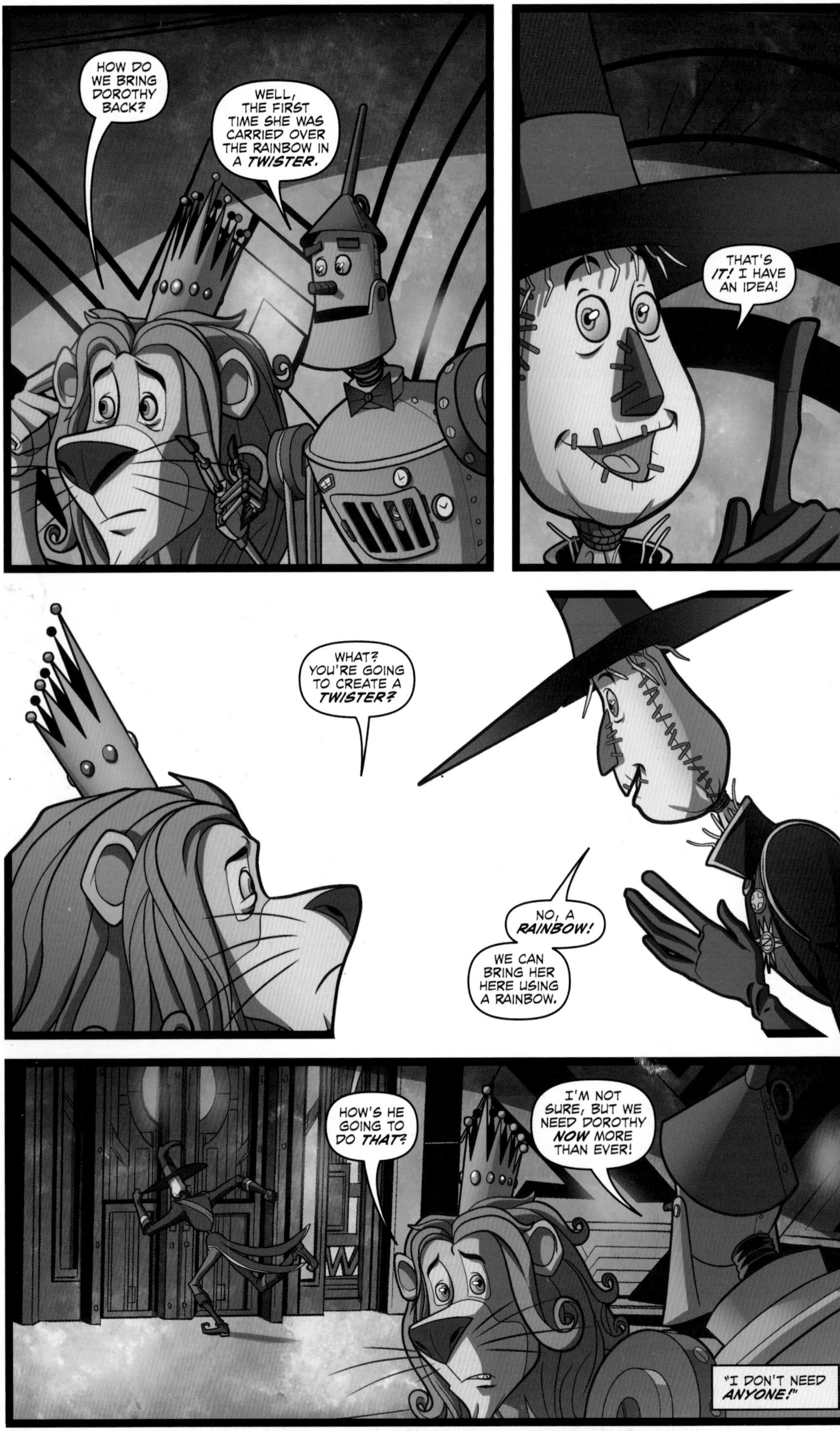

HOW DO WE BRING DOROTHY BACK?
WELL, THE FIRST TIME SHE WAS CARRIED OVER THE RAINBOW IN A *TWISTER.*
THAT'S *IT!* I HAVE AN IDEA!
WHAT? YOU'RE GOING TO CREATE A *TWISTER?*
NO, A *RAINBOW!*
WE CAN BRING HER HERE USING A RAINBOW.
HOW'S HE GOING TO DO *THAT?*
I'M NOT SURE, BUT WE NEED DOROTHY *NOW* MORE THAN EVER!
"I DON'T NEED *ANYONE!*"

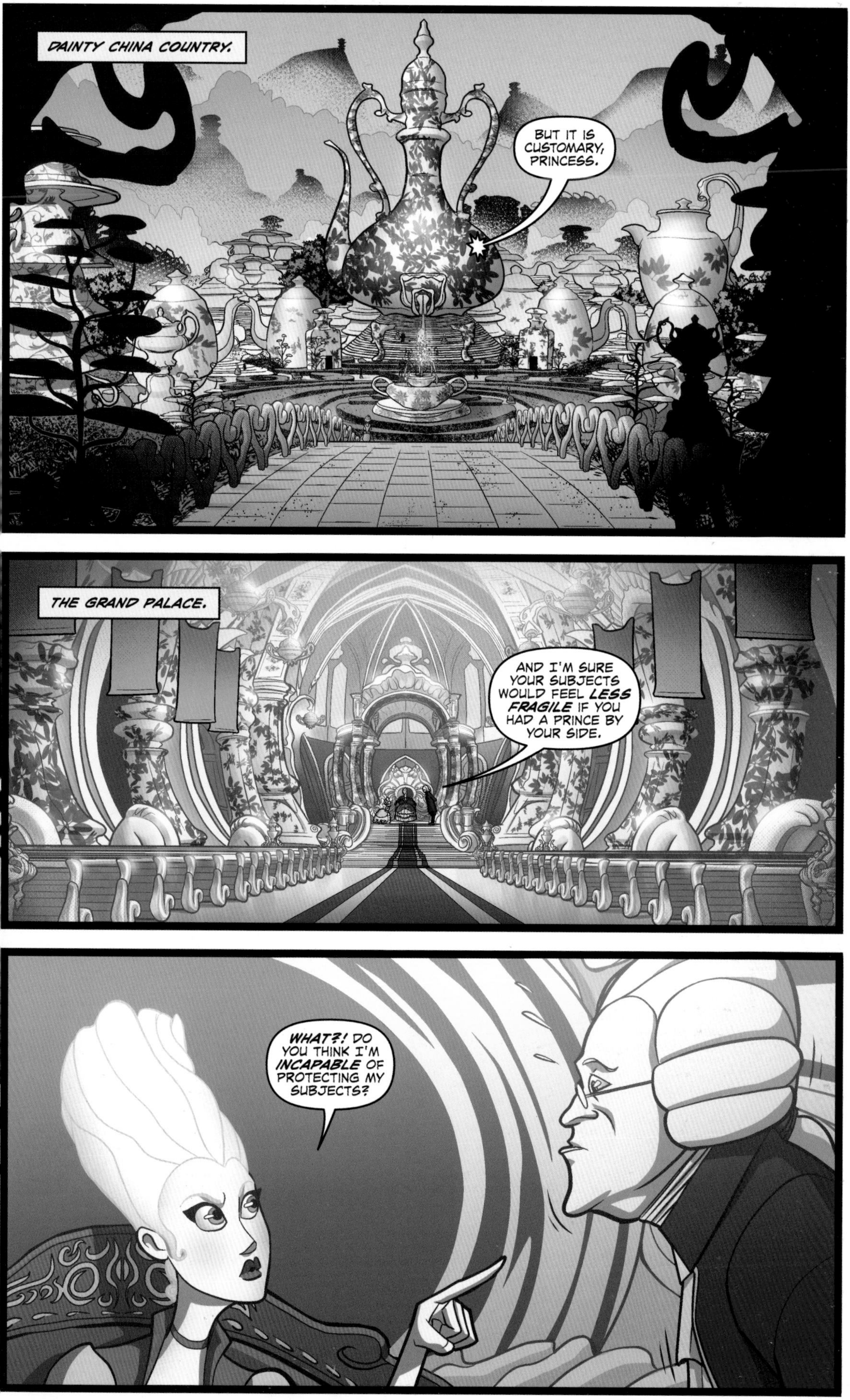
DAINTY CHINA COUNTRY.
BUT IT IS CUSTOMARY, PRINCESS.
THE GRAND PALACE.
AND I'M SURE YOUR SUBJECTS WOULD FEEL LESS FRAGILE IF YOU HAD A PRINCE BY YOUR SIDE.
WHAT?! DO YOU THINK I'M INCAPABLE OF PROTECTING MY SUBJECTS?

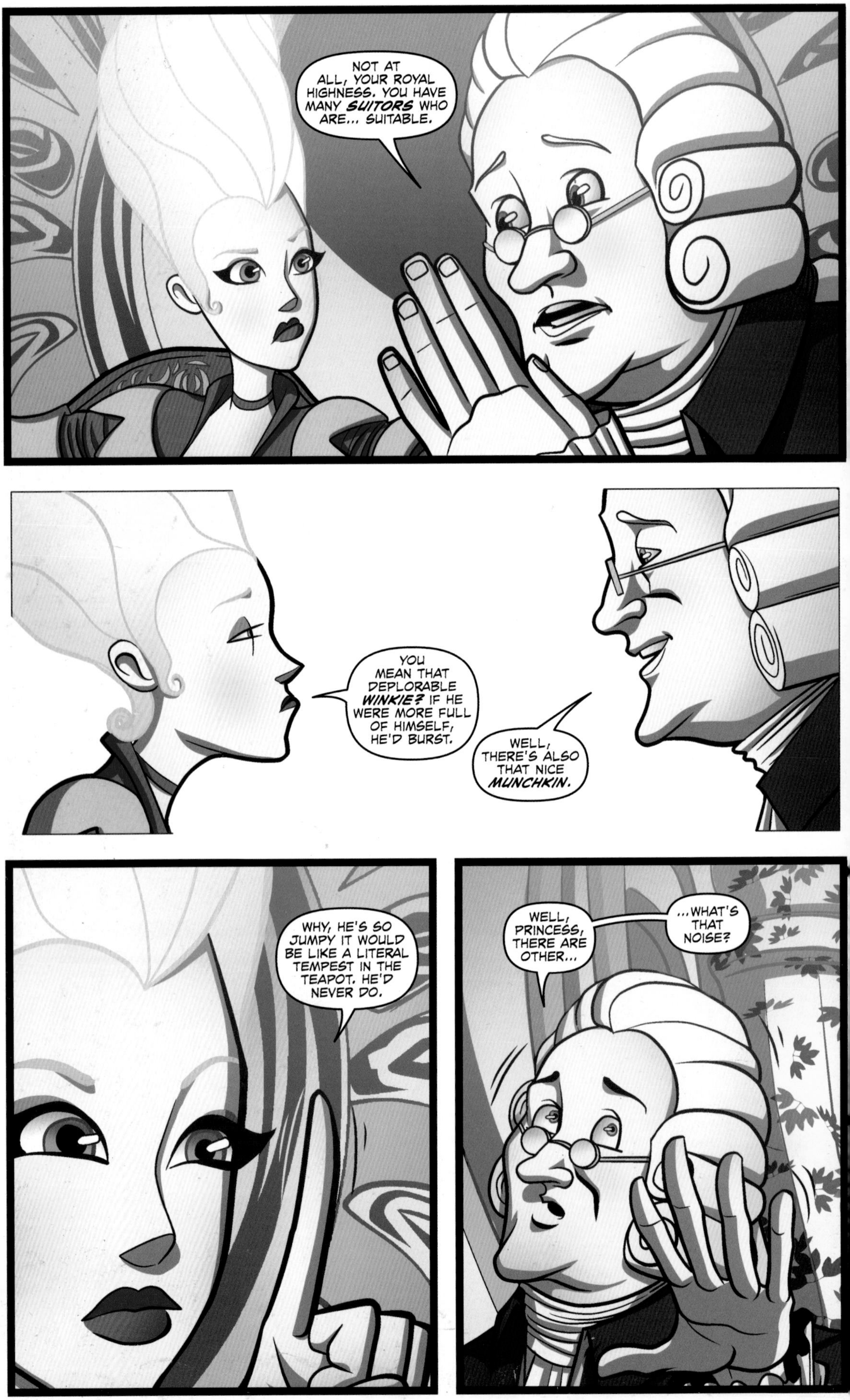
NOT AT ALL, YOUR ROYAL HIGHNESS. YOU HAVE MANY *SUITORS* WHO ARE... SUITABLE.
YOU MEAN THAT DEPLORABLE *WINKIE?* IF HE WERE MORE FULL OF HIMSELF, HE'D BURST.
WELL, THERE'S ALSO THAT NICE *MUNCHKIN.*
WHY, HE'S SO JUMPY IT WOULD BE LIKE A LITERAL TEMPEST IN THE TEAPOT. HE'D NEVER DO.
WELL, PRINCESS, THERE ARE OTHER...
...WHAT'S THAT NOISE?

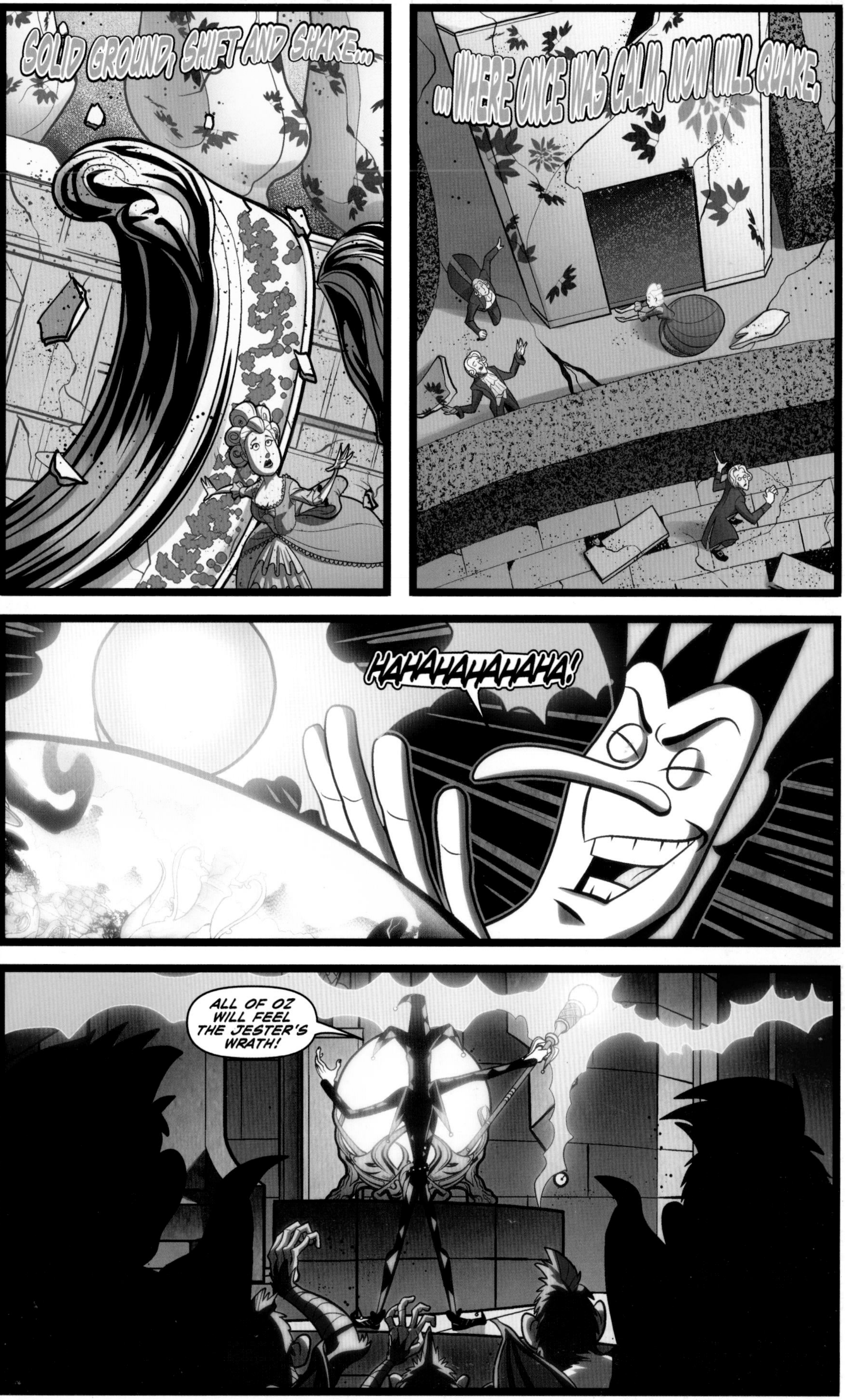
SOLID GROUND, SHIFT AND SHAKE...
...WHERE ONCE WAS CALM, NOW WILL QUAKE.
HAHAHAHAHAHA!
ALL OF OZ WILL FEEL THE JESTER'S WRATH!

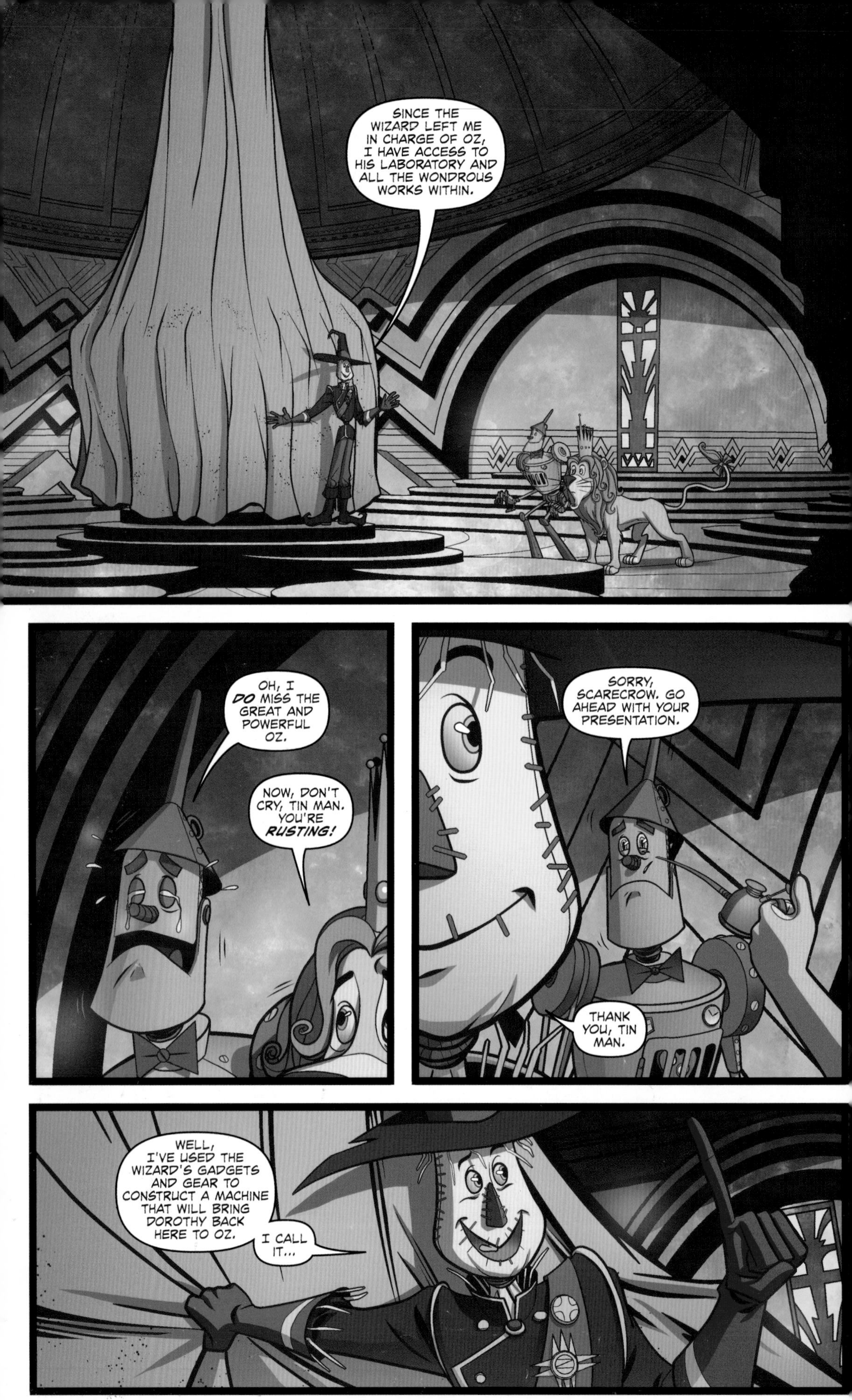
SINCE THE WIZARD LEFT ME IN CHARGE OF OZ, I HAVE ACCESS TO HIS LABORATORY AND ALL THE WONDROUS WORKS WITHIN.
OH, I *DO* MISS THE GREAT AND POWERFUL OZ.
NOW, DON'T CRY, TIN MAN. YOU'RE *RUSTING!*
SORRY, SCARECROW. GO AHEAD WITH YOUR PRESENTATION.
THANK YOU, TIN MAN.
WELL, I'VE USED THE WIZARD'S GADGETS AND GEAR TO CONSTRUCT A MACHINE THAT WILL BRING DOROTHY BACK HERE TO OZ.
I CALL IT...

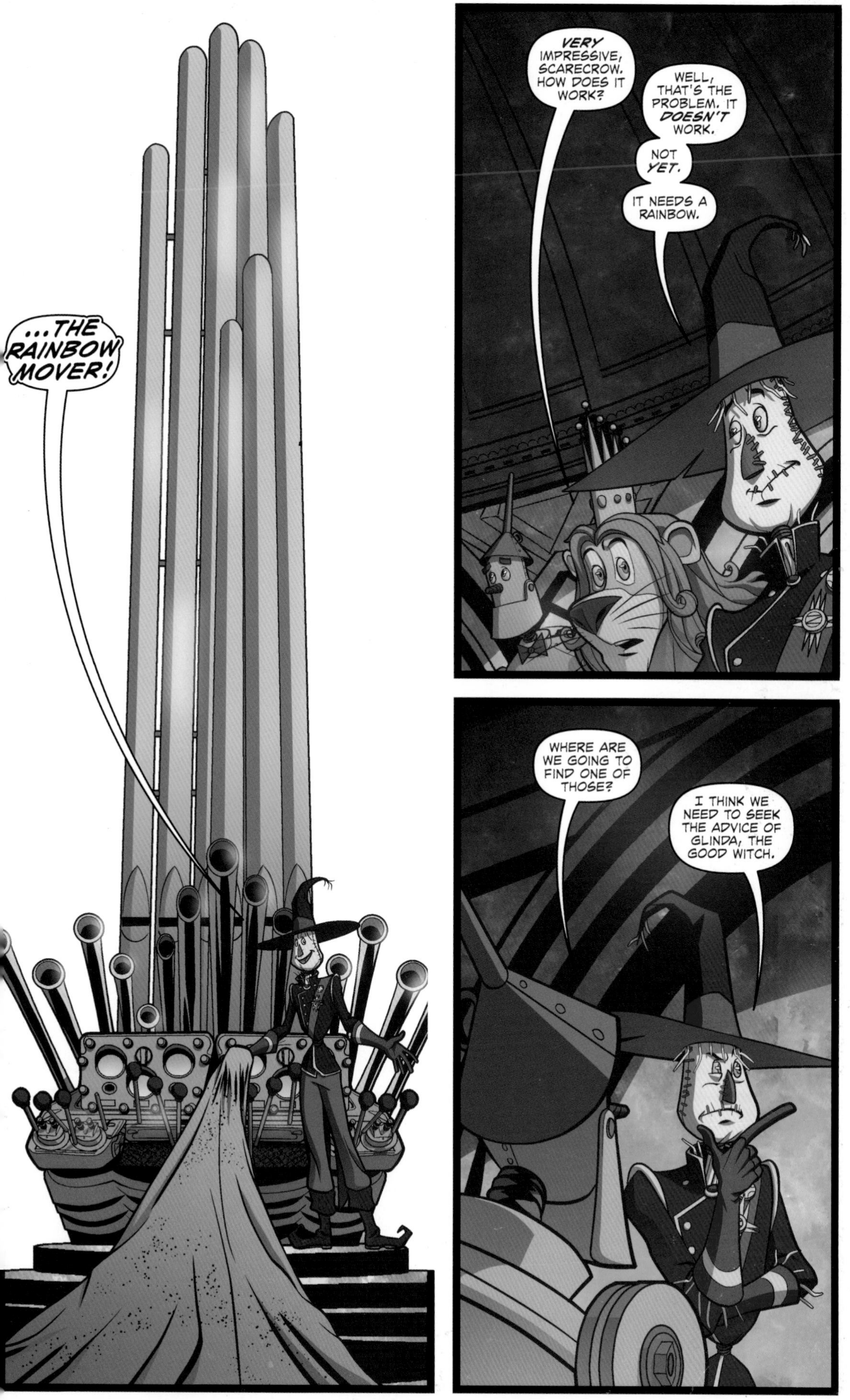
...THE RAINBOW MOVER!
VERY IMPRESSIVE, SCARECROW. HOW DOES IT WORK?
WELL, THAT'S THE PROBLEM. IT DOESN'T WORK.
NOT YET.
IT NEEDS A RAINBOW.
WHERE ARE WE GOING TO FIND ONE OF THOSE?
I THINK WE NEED TO SEEK THE ADVICE OF GLINDA, THE GOOD WITCH.

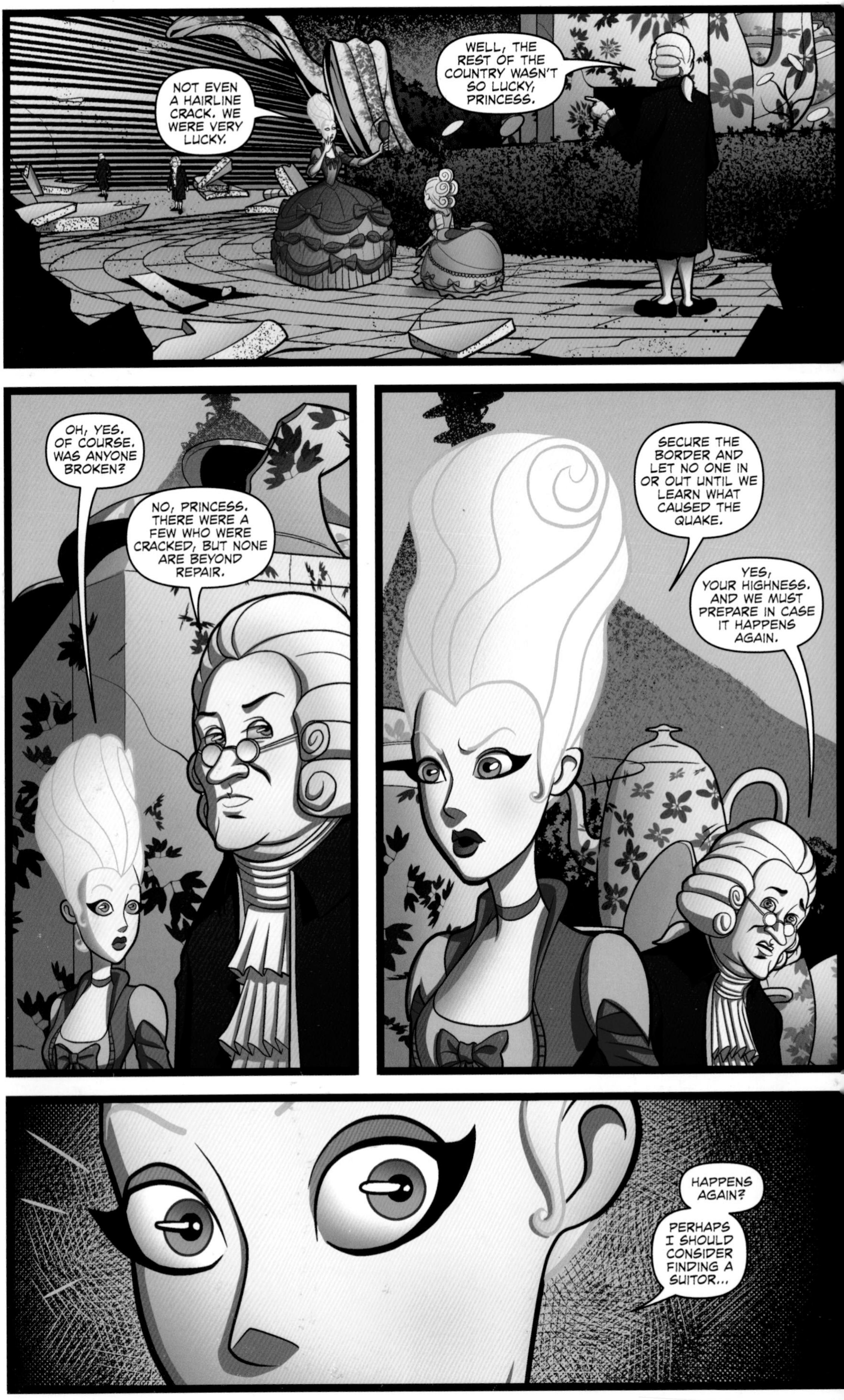
NOT EVEN A HAIRLINE CRACK. WE WERE VERY LUCKY.
WELL, THE REST OF THE COUNTRY WASN'T SO LUCKY, PRINCESS.
OH, YES. OF COURSE. WAS ANYONE BROKEN?
NO, PRINCESS. THERE WERE A FEW WHO WERE CRACKED, BUT NONE ARE BEYOND REPAIR.
SECURE THE BORDER AND LET NO ONE IN OR OUT UNTIL WE LEARN WHAT CAUSED THE QUAKE.
YES, YOUR HIGHNESS. AND WE MUST PREPARE IN CASE IT HAPPENS AGAIN.
HAPPENS AGAIN?
PERHAPS I SHOULD CONSIDER FINDING A SUITOR...

ONCE WE REACH GLINDA'S CASTLE, SHE'LL KNOW WHERE TO FIND A RAINBOW...

...BUT FIRST WE HAVE TO CROSS THE MUNCHKIN RIVER.

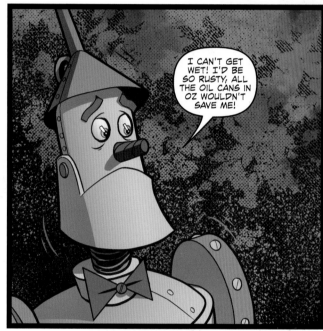

I CAN'T GET WET! I'D BE SO RUSTY, ALL THE OIL CANS IN OZ WOULDN'T SAVE ME!

WELL, WE DON'T HAVE A BOAT...

...PERHAPS WE CAN *SWING* ACROSS?

WELL, WE FOUND A TREE *TALL* ENOUGH, BUT WE STILL NEED *ROPE*.

WOULD A NICE, STRONG *VINE* WORK?

I THINK IT WOULD. WAIT. WHO SAID THAT?

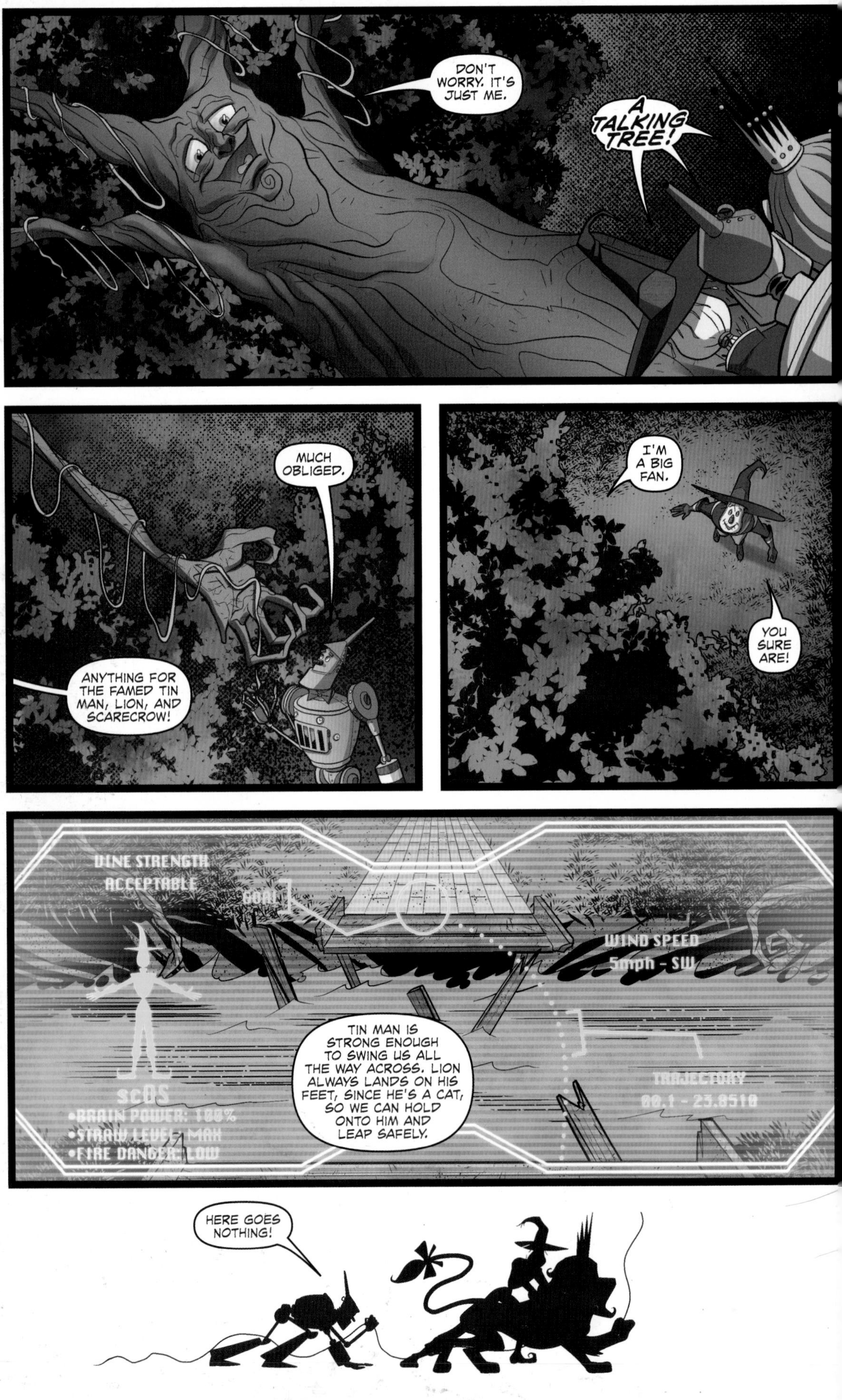
DON'T WORRY. IT'S JUST ME.
A TALKING TREE!
MUCH OBLIGED.
ANYTHING FOR THE FAMED TIN MAN, LION, AND SCARECROW!
I'M A BIG FAN.
YOU SURE ARE!
VINE STRENGTH ACCEPTABLE
GOAL
WIND SPEED 5mph - SW
scOS
•BRAIN POWER: 100%
•STRAW LEVEL: MAX
•FIRE DANGER: LOW
TIN MAN IS STRONG ENOUGH TO SWING US ALL THE WAY ACROSS. LION ALWAYS LANDS ON HIS FEET, SINCE HE'S A CAT, SO WE CAN HOLD ONTO HIM AND LEAP SAFELY.
TRAJECTORY 00.1 - 23.8510
HERE GOES NOTHING!

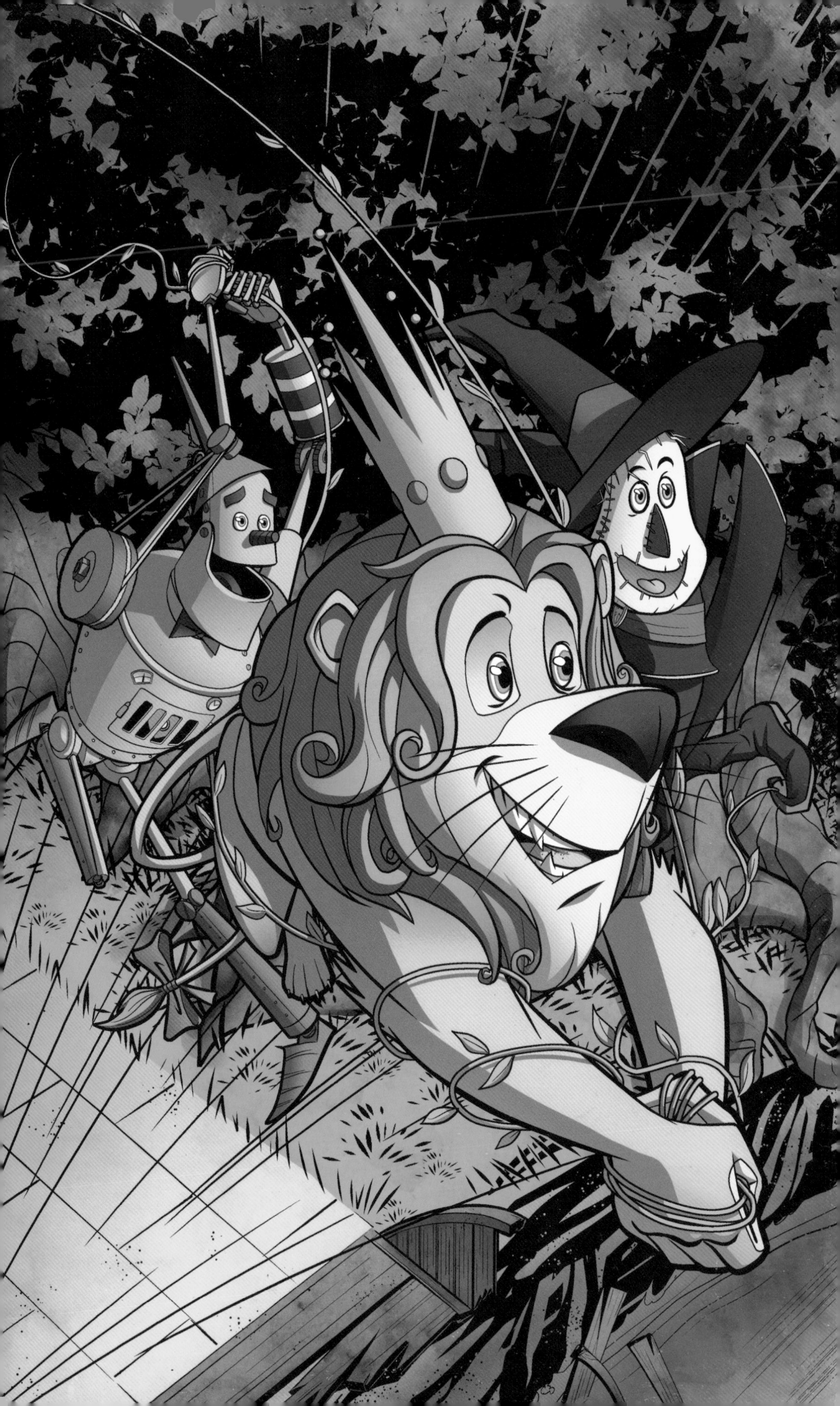

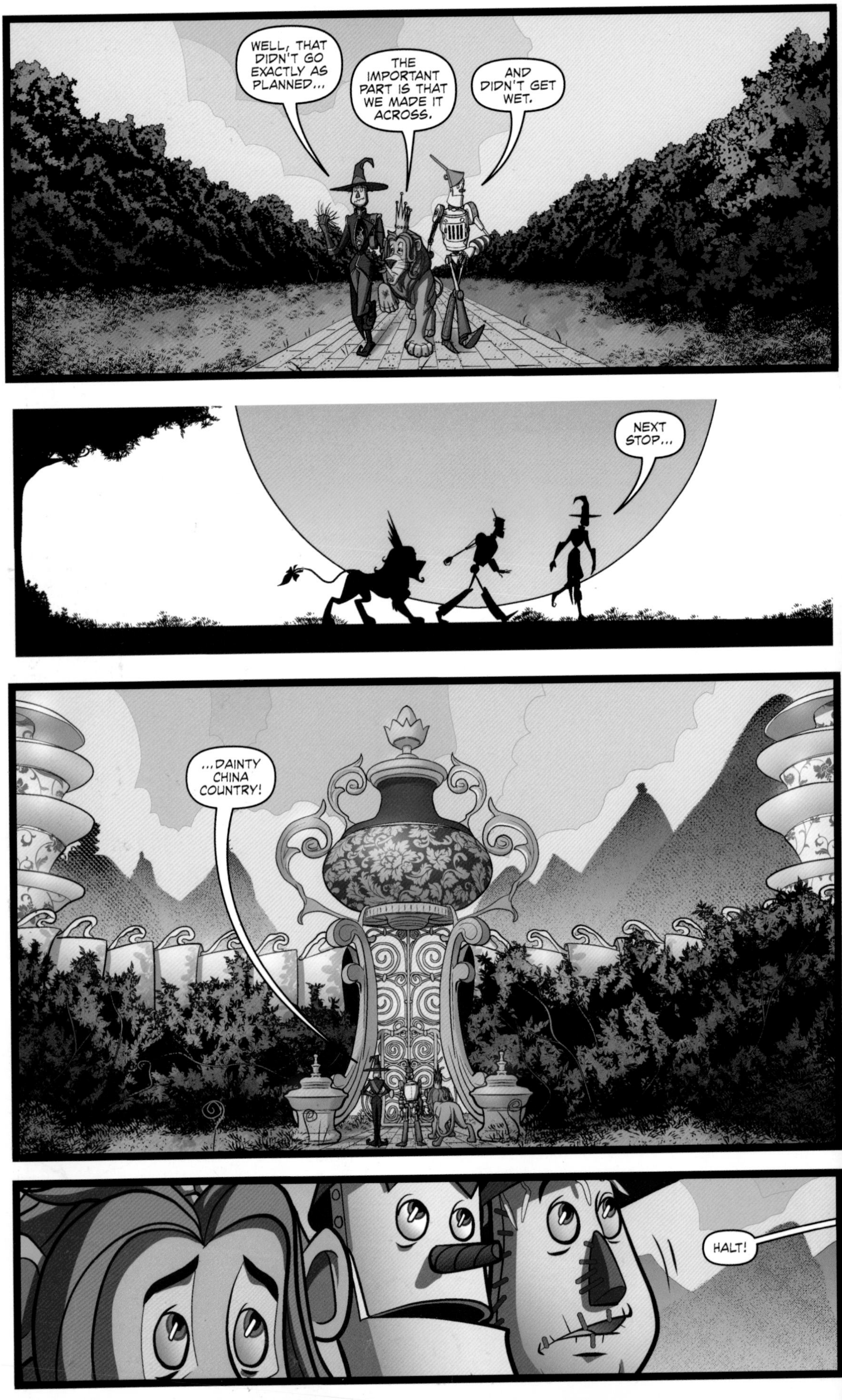
WELL, THAT DIDN'T GO EXACTLY AS PLANNED...
THE IMPORTANT PART IS THAT WE MADE IT ACROSS.
AND DIDN'T GET WET.
NEXT STOP...
...DAINTY CHINA COUNTRY!
HALT!

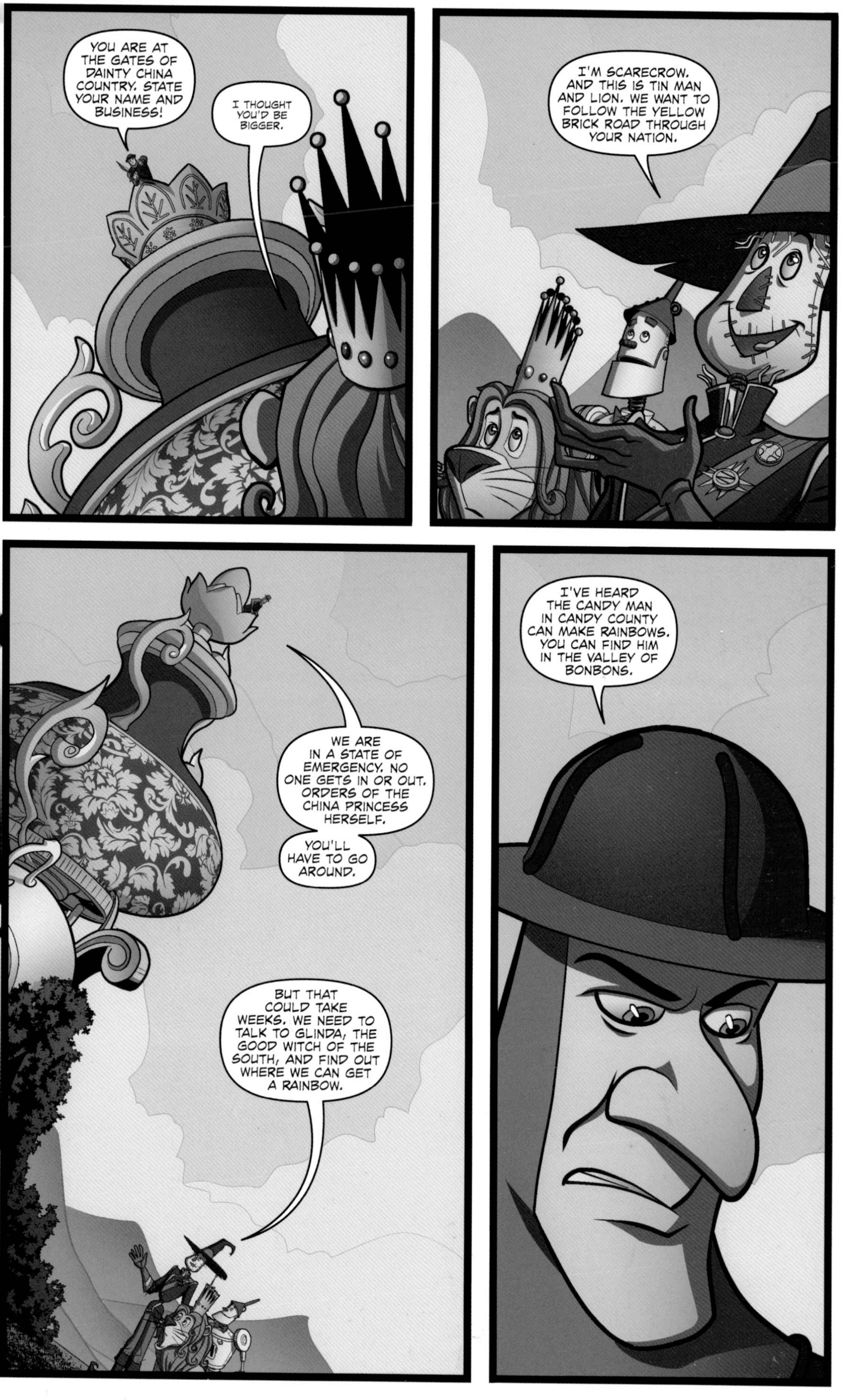
YOU ARE AT THE GATES OF DAINTY CHINA COUNTRY. STATE YOUR NAME AND BUSINESS!
I THOUGHT YOU'D BE BIGGER.
I'M SCARECROW. AND THIS IS TIN MAN AND LION. WE WANT TO FOLLOW THE YELLOW BRICK ROAD THROUGH YOUR NATION.
WE ARE IN A STATE OF EMERGENCY. NO ONE GETS IN OR OUT. ORDERS OF THE CHINA PRINCESS HERSELF.
YOU'LL HAVE TO GO AROUND.
BUT THAT COULD TAKE WEEKS. WE NEED TO TALK TO GLINDA, THE GOOD WITCH OF THE SOUTH, AND FIND OUT WHERE WE CAN GET A RAINBOW.
I'VE HEARD THE CANDY MAN IN CANDY COUNTY CAN MAKE RAINBOWS. YOU CAN FIND HIM IN THE VALLEY OF BONBONS.

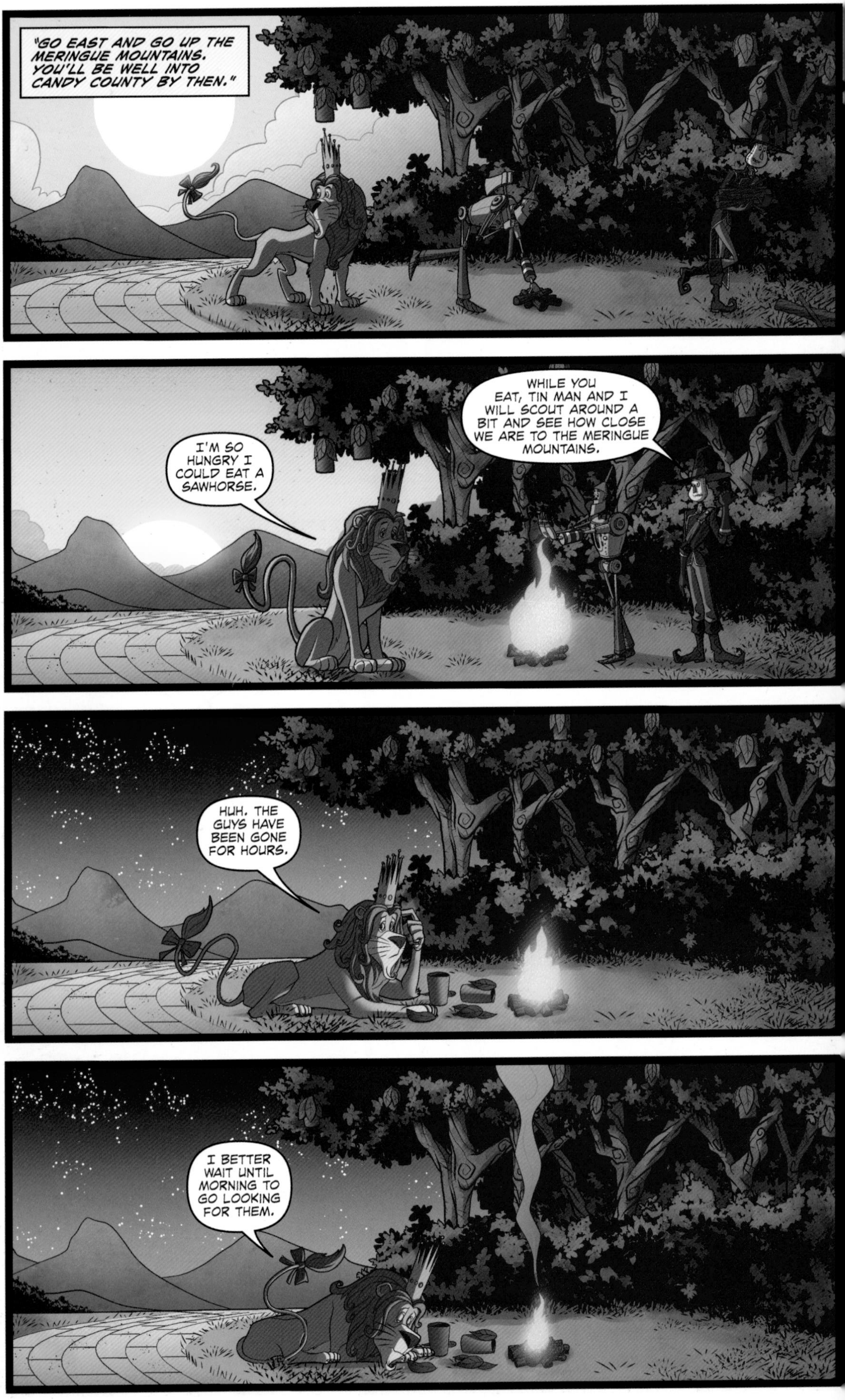
"GO EAST AND GO UP THE MERINGUE MOUNTAINS. YOU'LL BE WELL INTO CANDY COUNTY BY THEN."
I'M SO HUNGRY I COULD EAT A SAWHORSE.
WHILE YOU EAT, TIN MAN AND I WILL SCOUT AROUND A BIT AND SEE HOW CLOSE WE ARE TO THE MERINGUE MOUNTAINS.
HUH. THE GUYS HAVE BEEN GONE FOR HOURS.
I BETTER WAIT UNTIL MORNING TO GO LOOKING FOR THEM.

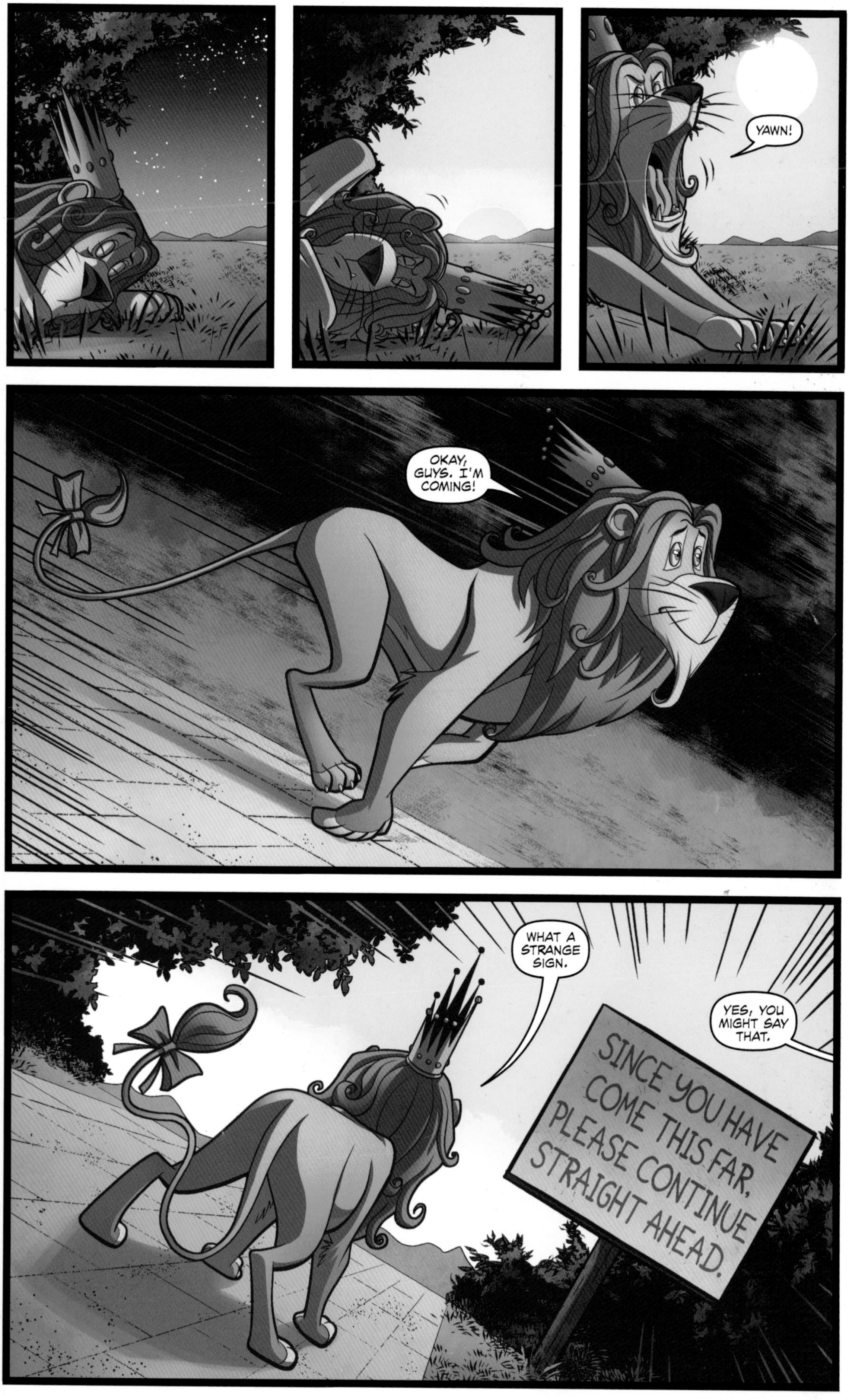
YAWN!
OKAY, GUYS. I'M COMING!
WHAT A STRANGE SIGN.
SINCE YOU HAVE COME THIS FAR, PLEASE CONTINUE STRAIGHT AHEAD.
YES, YOU MIGHT SAY THAT.

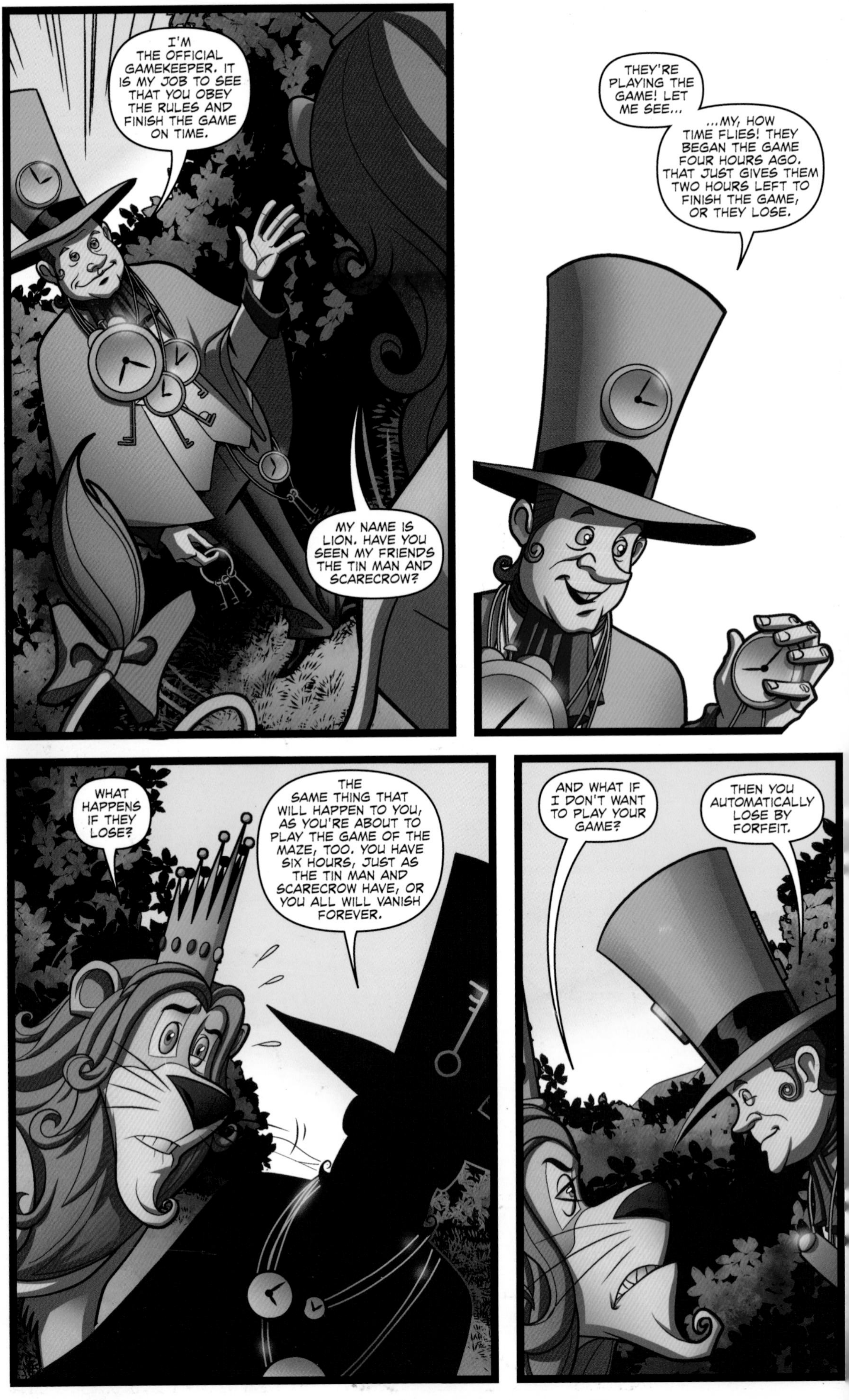

I'M THE OFFICIAL GAMEKEEPER. IT IS MY JOB TO SEE THAT YOU OBEY THE RULES AND FINISH THE GAME ON TIME.
MY NAME IS LION. HAVE YOU SEEN MY FRIENDS THE TIN MAN AND SCARECROW?
THEY'RE PLAYING THE GAME! LET ME SEE...
...MY, HOW TIME FLIES! THEY BEGAN THE GAME FOUR HOURS AGO. THAT JUST GIVES THEM TWO HOURS LEFT TO FINISH THE GAME, OR THEY LOSE.
WHAT HAPPENS IF THEY LOSE?
THE SAME THING THAT WILL HAPPEN TO YOU, AS YOU'RE ABOUT TO PLAY THE GAME OF THE MAZE, TOO. YOU HAVE SIX HOURS, JUST AS THE TIN MAN AND SCARECROW HAVE, OR YOU ALL WILL VANISH FOREVER.
AND WHAT IF I DON'T WANT TO PLAY YOUR GAME?
THEN YOU AUTOMATICALLY LOSE BY FORFEIT.

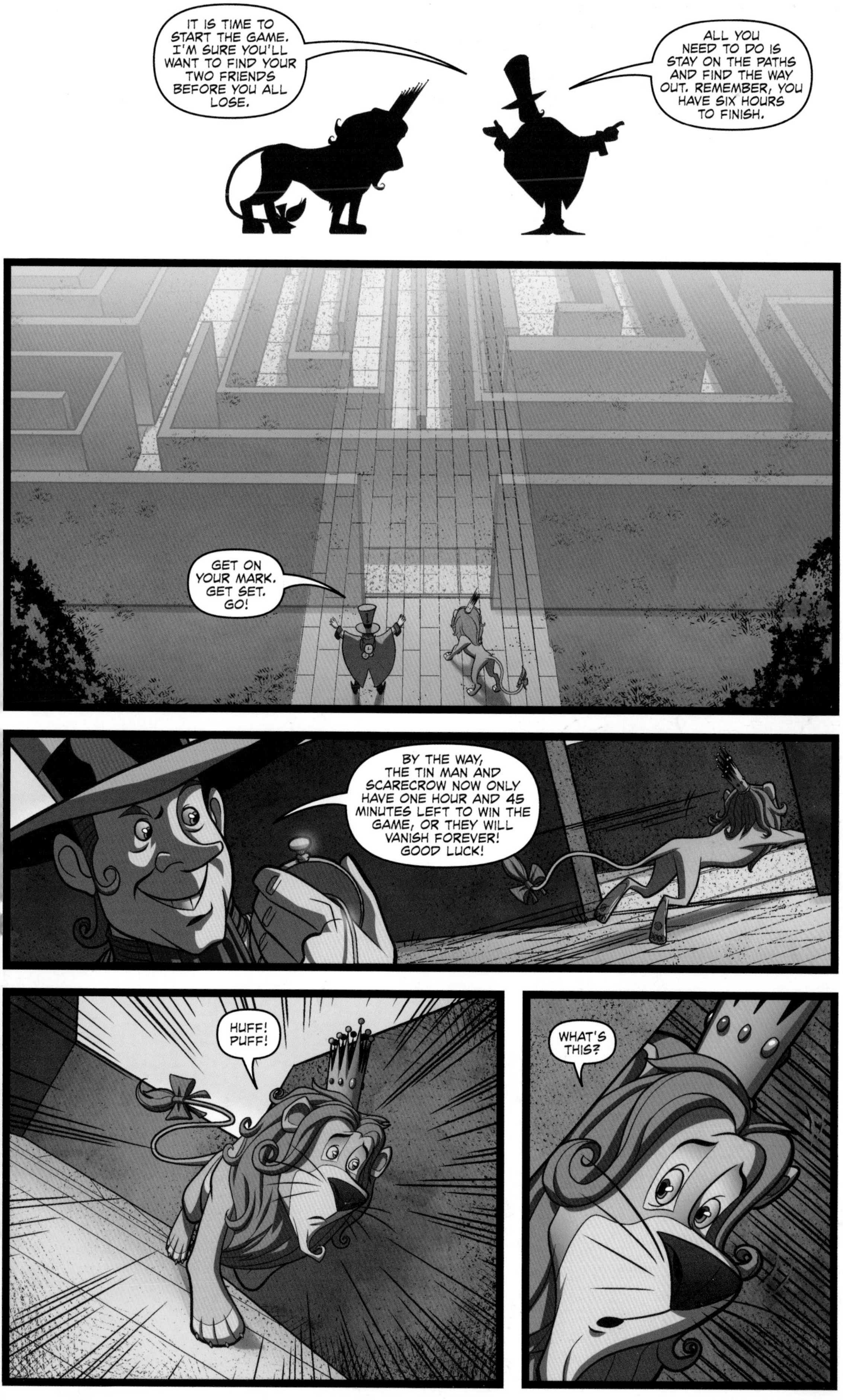
IT IS TIME TO START THE GAME. I'M SURE YOU'LL WANT TO FIND YOUR TWO FRIENDS BEFORE YOU ALL LOSE.
ALL YOU NEED TO DO IS STAY ON THE PATHS AND FIND THE WAY OUT. REMEMBER, YOU HAVE SIX HOURS TO FINISH.
GET ON YOUR MARK. GET SET. GO!
BY THE WAY, THE TIN MAN AND SCARECROW NOW ONLY HAVE ONE HOUR AND 45 MINUTES LEFT TO WIN THE GAME, OR THEY WILL VANISH FOREVER! GOOD LUCK!
HUFF! PUFF!
WHAT'S THIS?

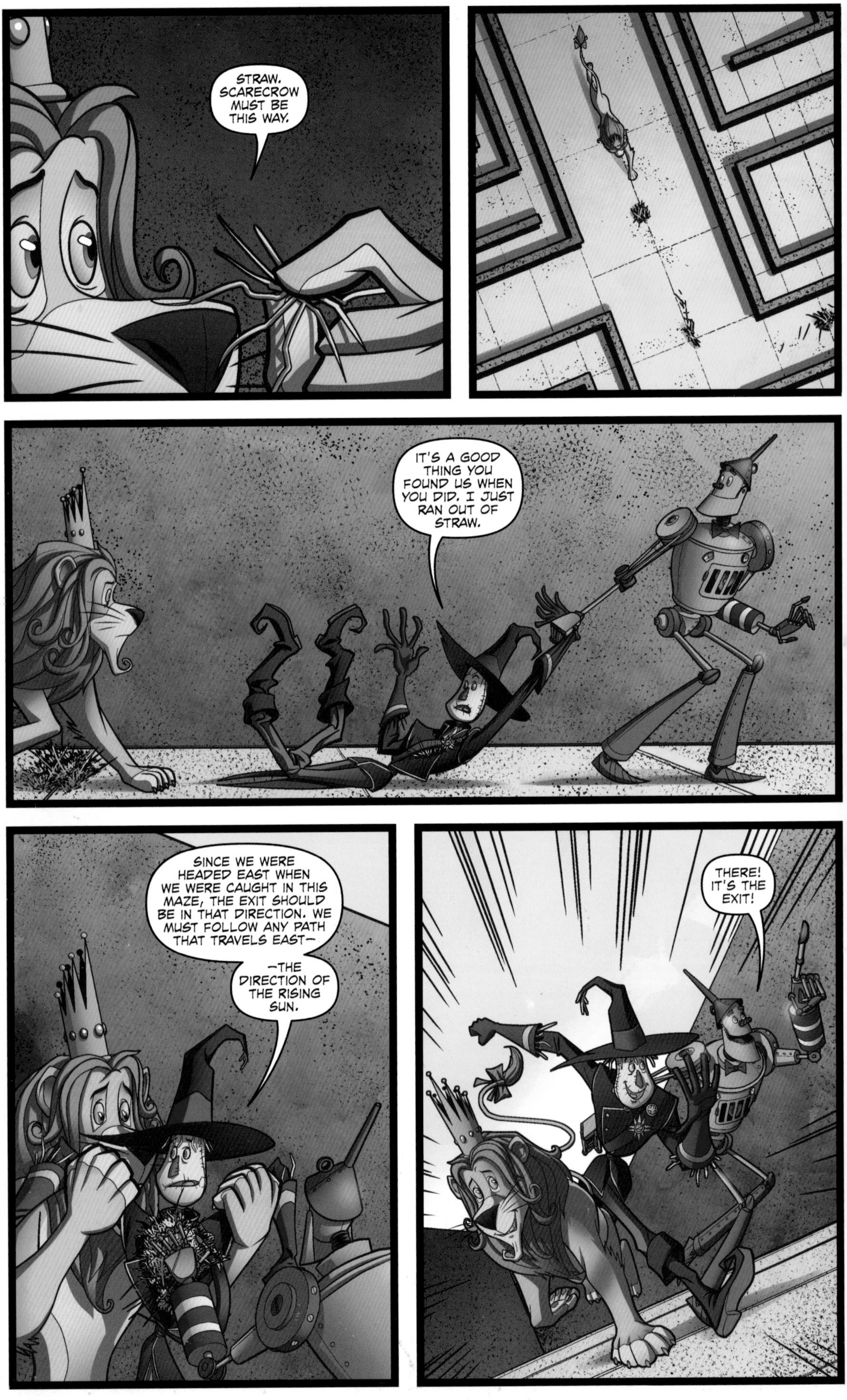

STRAW. SCARECROW MUST BE THIS WAY.
IT'S A GOOD THING YOU FOUND US WHEN YOU DID. I JUST RAN OUT OF STRAW.
SINCE WE WERE HEADED EAST WHEN WE WERE CAUGHT IN THIS MAZE, THE EXIT SHOULD BE IN THAT DIRECTION. WE MUST FOLLOW ANY PATH THAT TRAVELS EAST—
—THE DIRECTION OF THE RISING SUN.
THERE! IT'S THE EXIT!

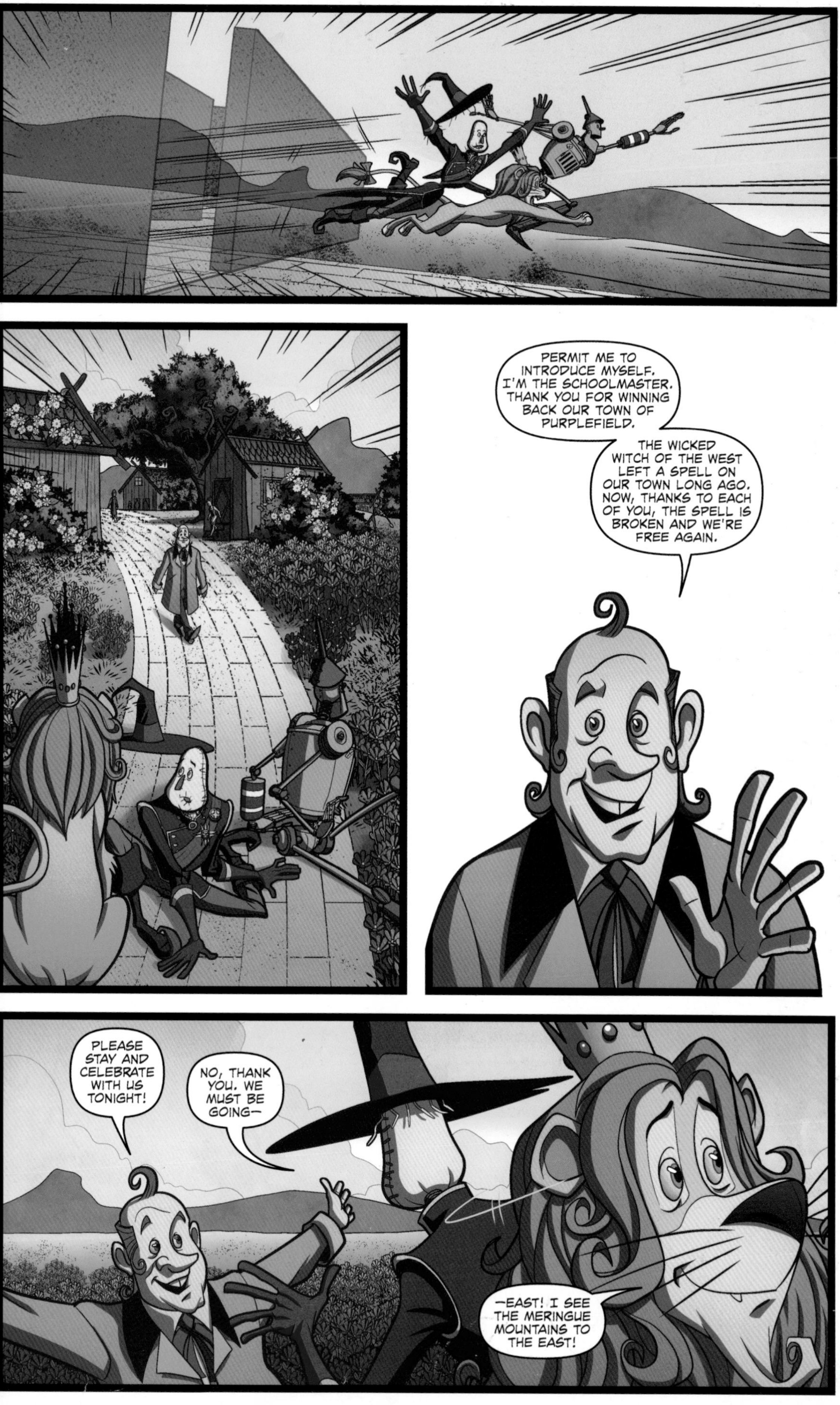

PERMIT ME TO INTRODUCE MYSELF. I'M THE SCHOOLMASTER. THANK YOU FOR WINNING BACK OUR TOWN OF PURPLEFIELD.
THE WICKED WITCH OF THE WEST LEFT A SPELL ON OUR TOWN LONG AGO. NOW, THANKS TO EACH OF YOU, THE SPELL IS BROKEN AND WE'RE FREE AGAIN.
PLEASE STAY AND CELEBRATE WITH US TONIGHT!
NO, THANK YOU. WE MUST BE GOING—
—EAST! I SEE THE MERINGUE MOUNTAINS TO THE EAST!

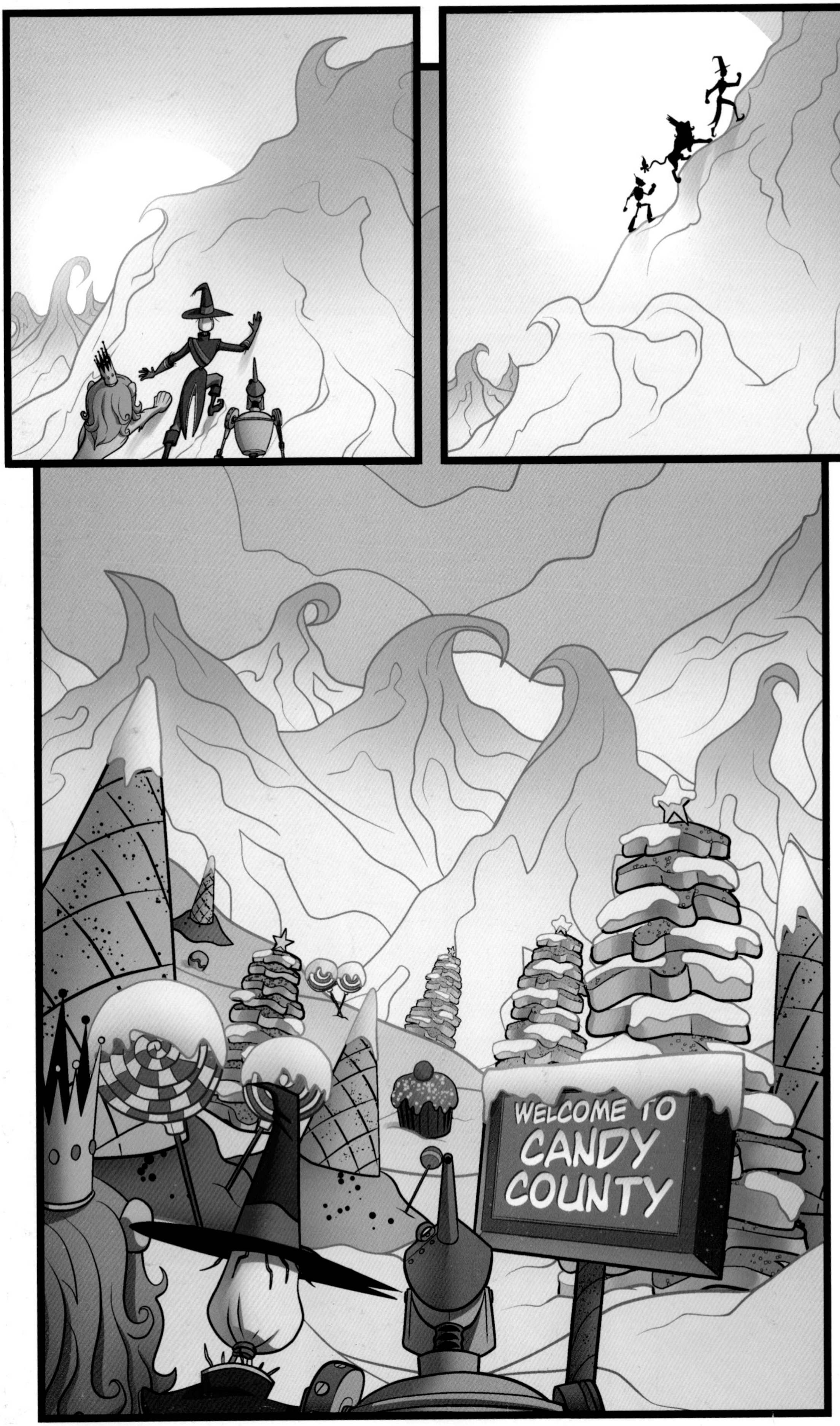
WELCOME TO
CANDY
COUNTY

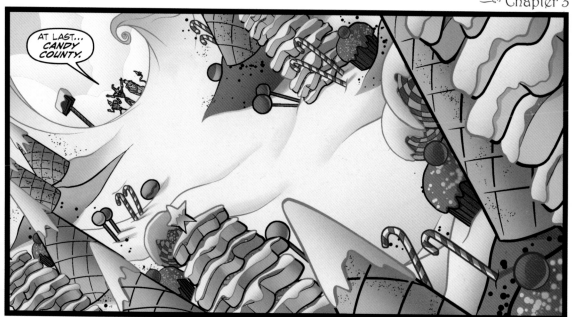

Chapter 3

AT LAST... CANDY COUNTY.

IT'S JUST BEAUTIFUL...

WHY ARE YOU GETTING ALL CHOKED UP, TIN MAN? YOU DON'T EVEN EAT CANDY. OR ANYTHING ELSE, FOR THAT MATTER.

COME ON, GUYS. I THINK THIS IS THE *VALLEY OF BONBONS*, WHERE WE'LL FIND THE *CANDY MAN.*

I SURE COULD GO FOR SOME BREAKFAST FIRST...

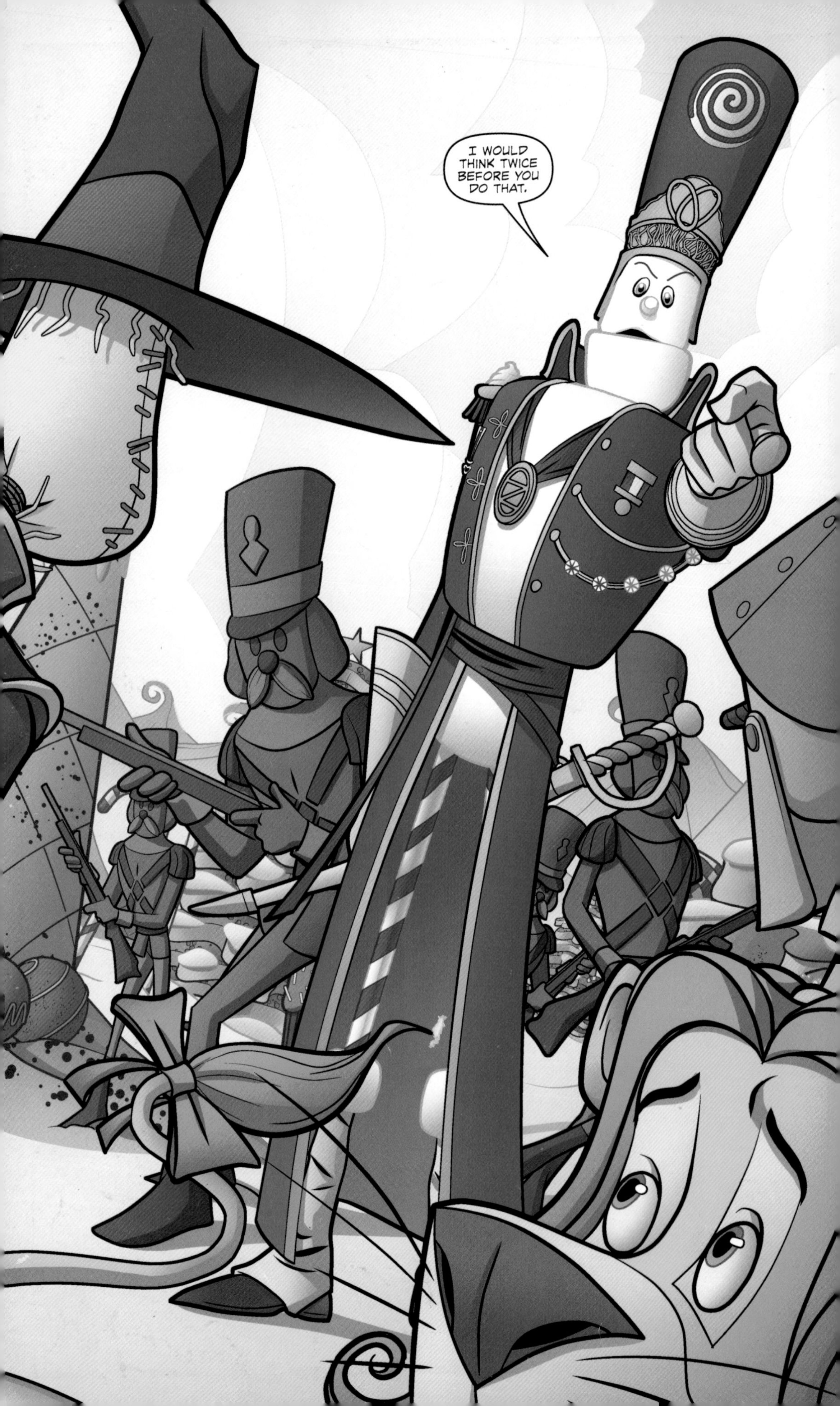
I WOULD THINK TWICE BEFORE YOU DO THAT.

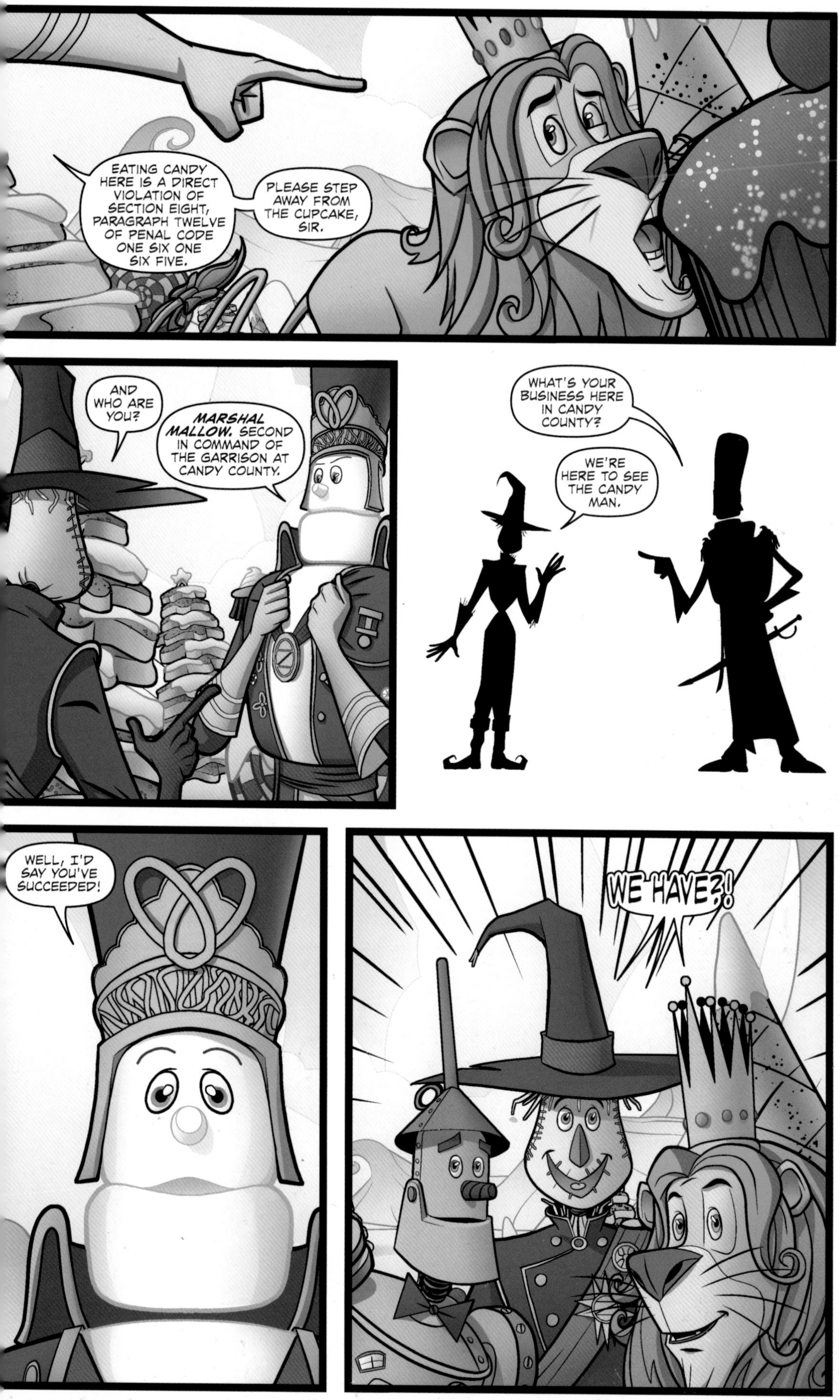
EATING CANDY HERE IS A DIRECT VIOLATION OF SECTION EIGHT, PARAGRAPH TWELVE OF PENAL CODE ONE SIX ONE SIX FIVE.
PLEASE STEP AWAY FROM THE CUPCAKE, SIR.
AND WHO ARE YOU?
MARSHAL MALLOW. SECOND IN COMMAND OF THE GARRISON AT CANDY COUNTY.
WHAT'S YOUR BUSINESS HERE IN CANDY COUNTY?
WE'RE HERE TO SEE THE CANDY MAN.
WELL, I'D SAY YOU'VE SUCCEEDED!
WE HAVE?!

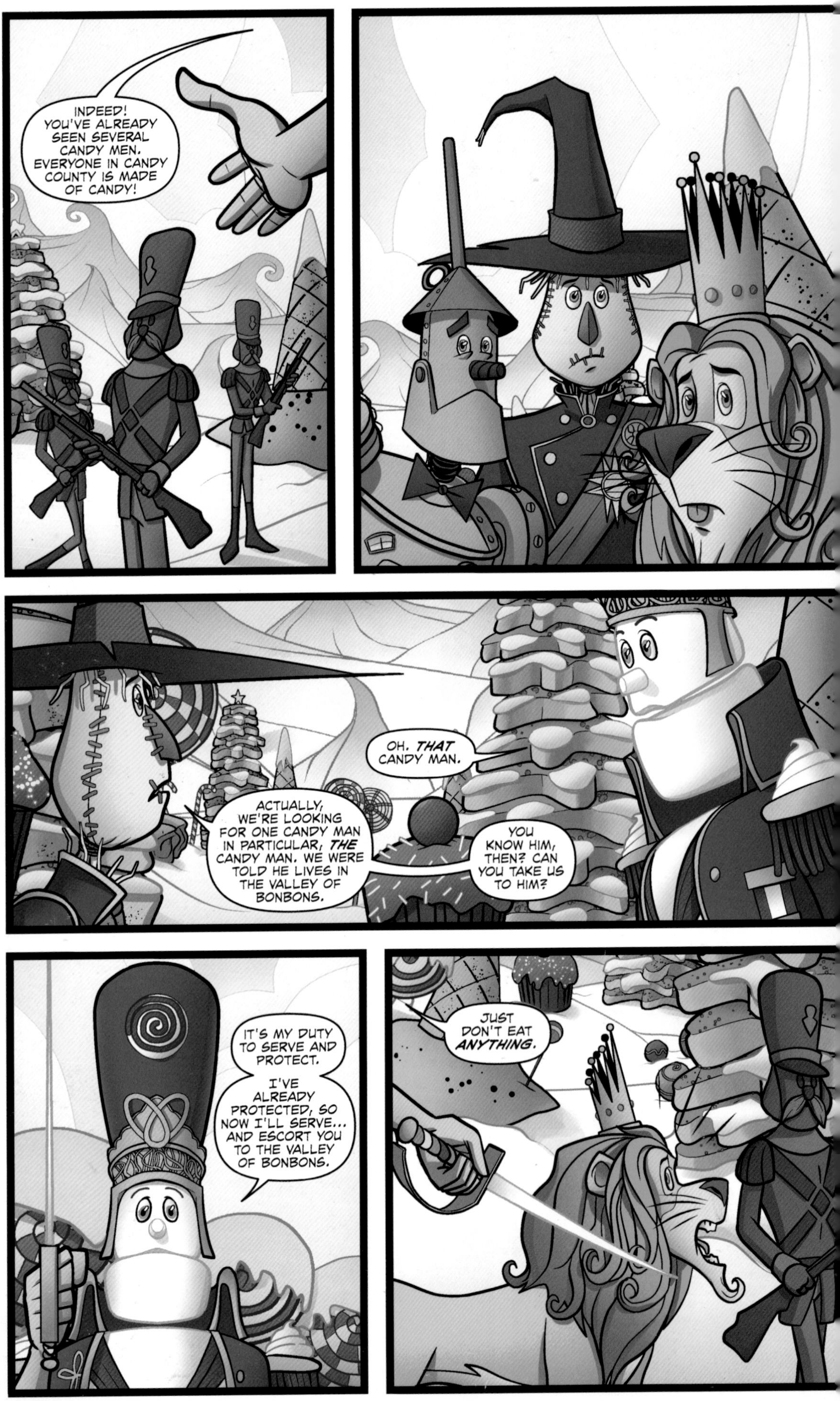
INDEED! YOU'VE ALREADY SEEN SEVERAL CANDY MEN. EVERYONE IN CANDY COUNTY IS MADE OF CANDY!
OH. *THAT* CANDY MAN.
ACTUALLY, WE'RE LOOKING FOR ONE CANDY MAN IN PARTICULAR, *THE* CANDY MAN. WE WERE TOLD HE LIVES IN THE VALLEY OF BONBONS.
YOU KNOW HIM, THEN? CAN YOU TAKE US TO HIM?
IT'S MY DUTY TO SERVE AND PROTECT.
I'VE ALREADY PROTECTED, SO NOW I'LL SERVE... AND ESCORT YOU TO THE VALLEY OF BONBONS.
JUST DON'T EAT *ANYTHING*.

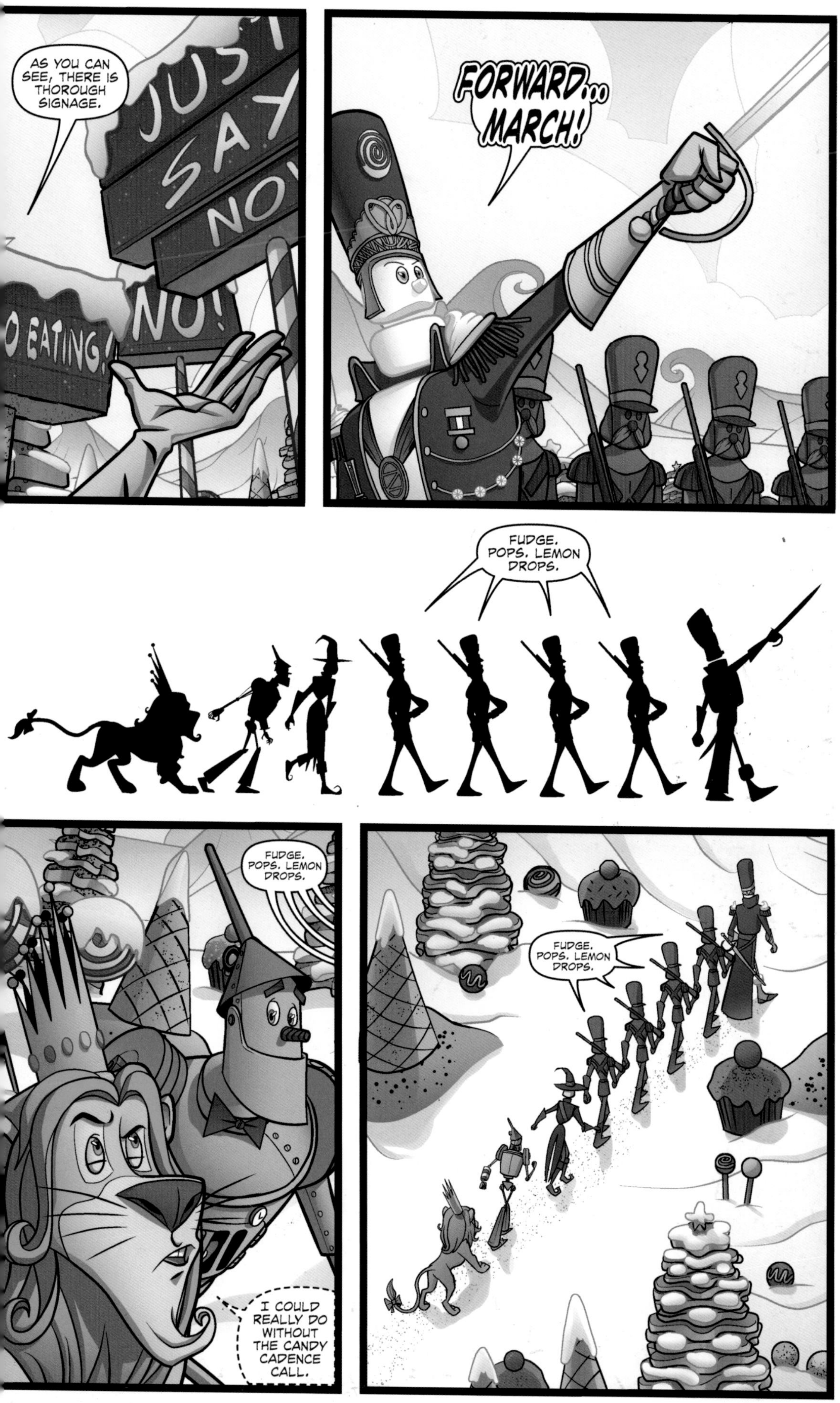
AS YOU CAN SEE, THERE IS THOROUGH SIGNAGE.
JUST SAY NO!
NO!
O EATING!
FORWARD... MARCH!
FUDGE. POPS. LEMON DROPS.
FUDGE. POPS. LEMON DROPS.
I COULD REALLY DO WITHOUT THE CANDY CADENCE CALL.
FUDGE. POPS. LEMON DROPS.

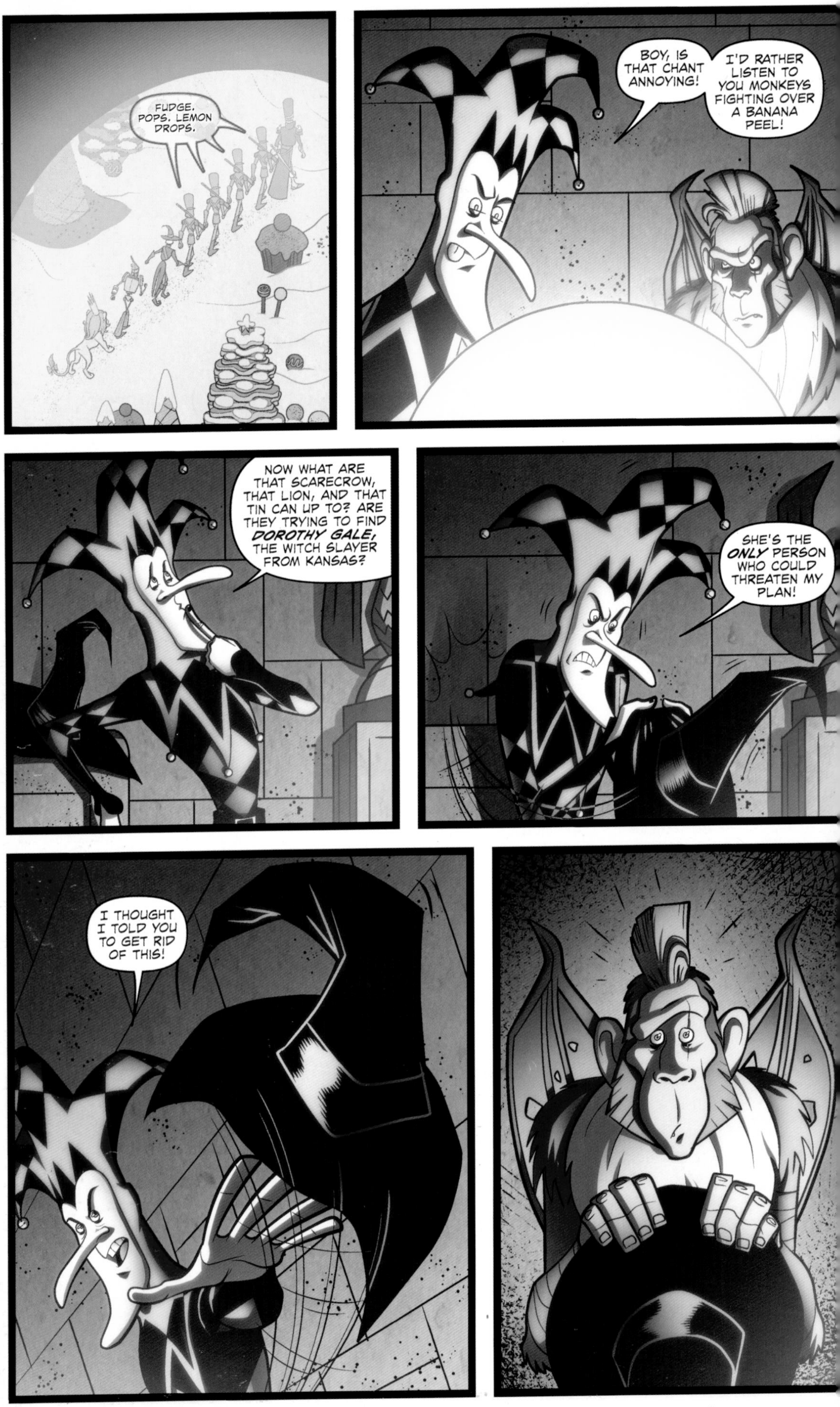
FUDGE. POPS. LEMON DROPS.
BOY, IS THAT CHANT ANNOYING!
I'D RATHER LISTEN TO YOU MONKEYS FIGHTING OVER A BANANA PEEL!
NOW WHAT ARE THAT SCARECROW, THAT LION, AND THAT TIN CAN UP TO? ARE THEY TRYING TO FIND DOROTHY GALE, THE WITCH SLAYER FROM KANSAS?
SHE'S THE ONLY PERSON WHO COULD THREATEN MY PLAN!
I THOUGHT I TOLD YOU TO GET RID OF THIS!

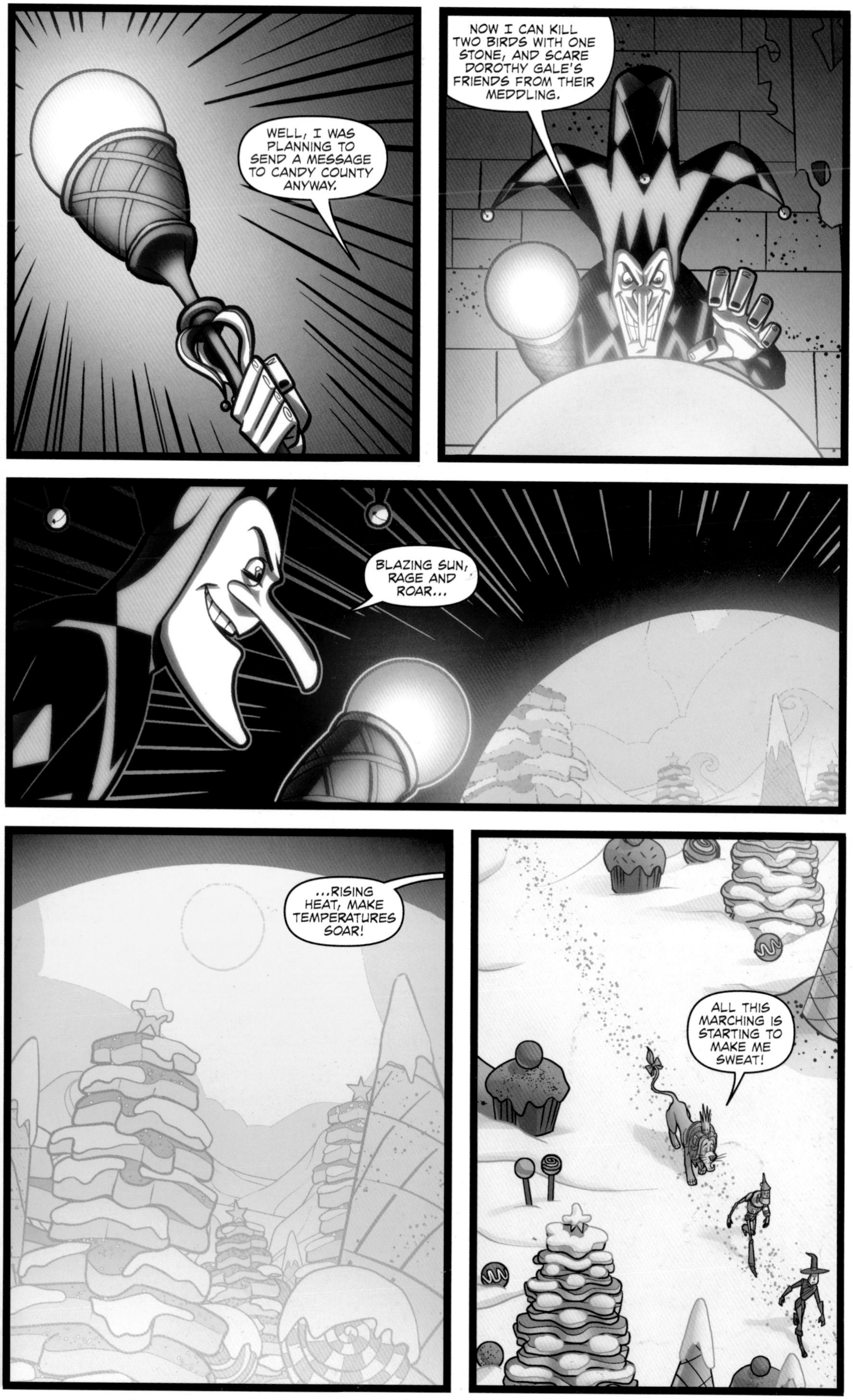

WELL, I WAS PLANNING TO SEND A MESSAGE TO CANDY COUNTY ANYWAY.
NOW I CAN KILL TWO BIRDS WITH ONE STONE, AND SCARE DOROTHY GALE'S FRIENDS FROM THEIR MEDDLING.
BLAZING SUN, RAGE AND ROAR...
...RISING HEAT, MAKE TEMPERATURES SOAR!
ALL THIS MARCHING IS STARTING TO MAKE ME SWEAT!

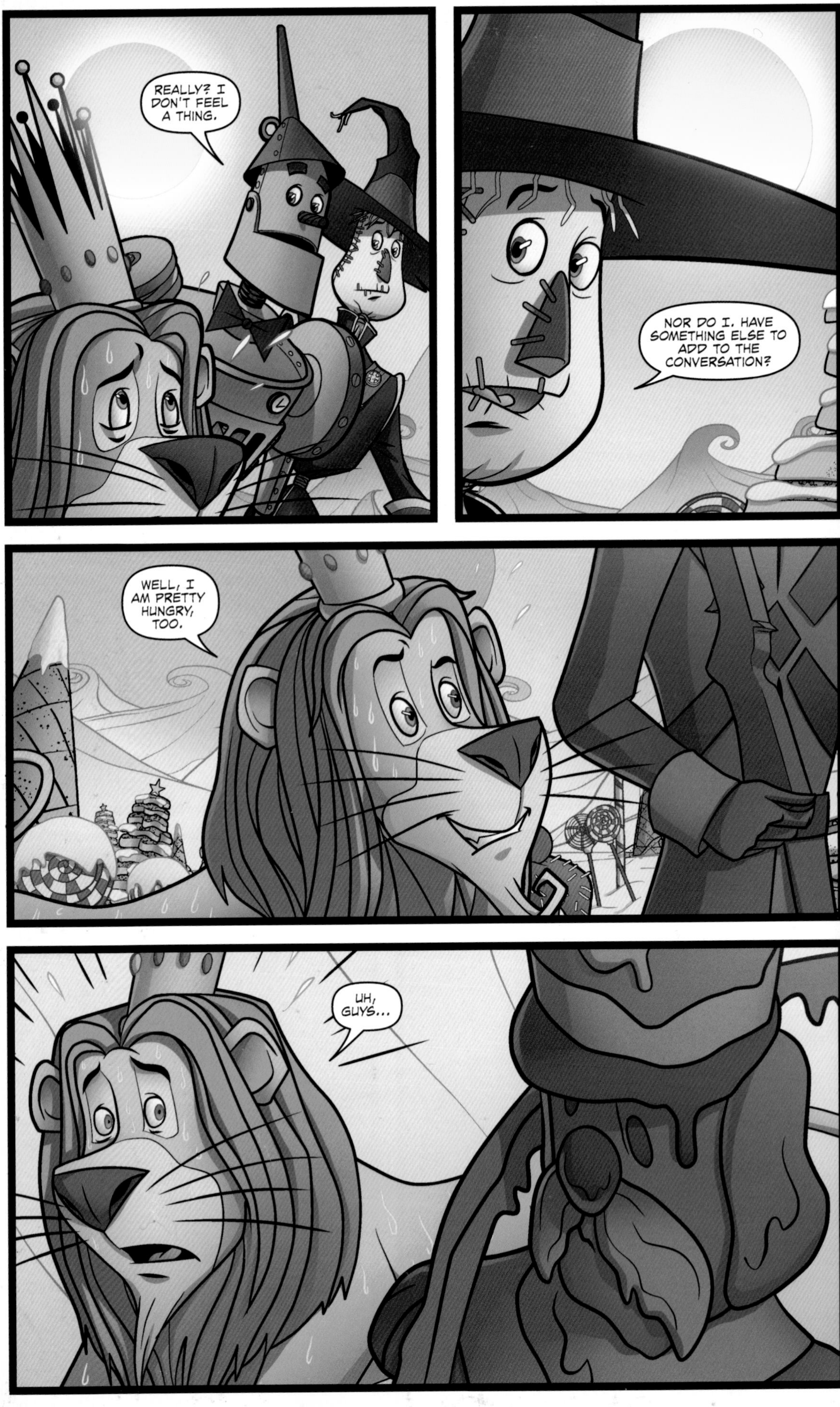
REALLY? I DON'T FEEL A THING.
NOR DO I. HAVE SOMETHING ELSE TO ADD TO THE CONVERSATION?
WELL, I AM PRETTY HUNGRY, TOO.
UH, GUYS...

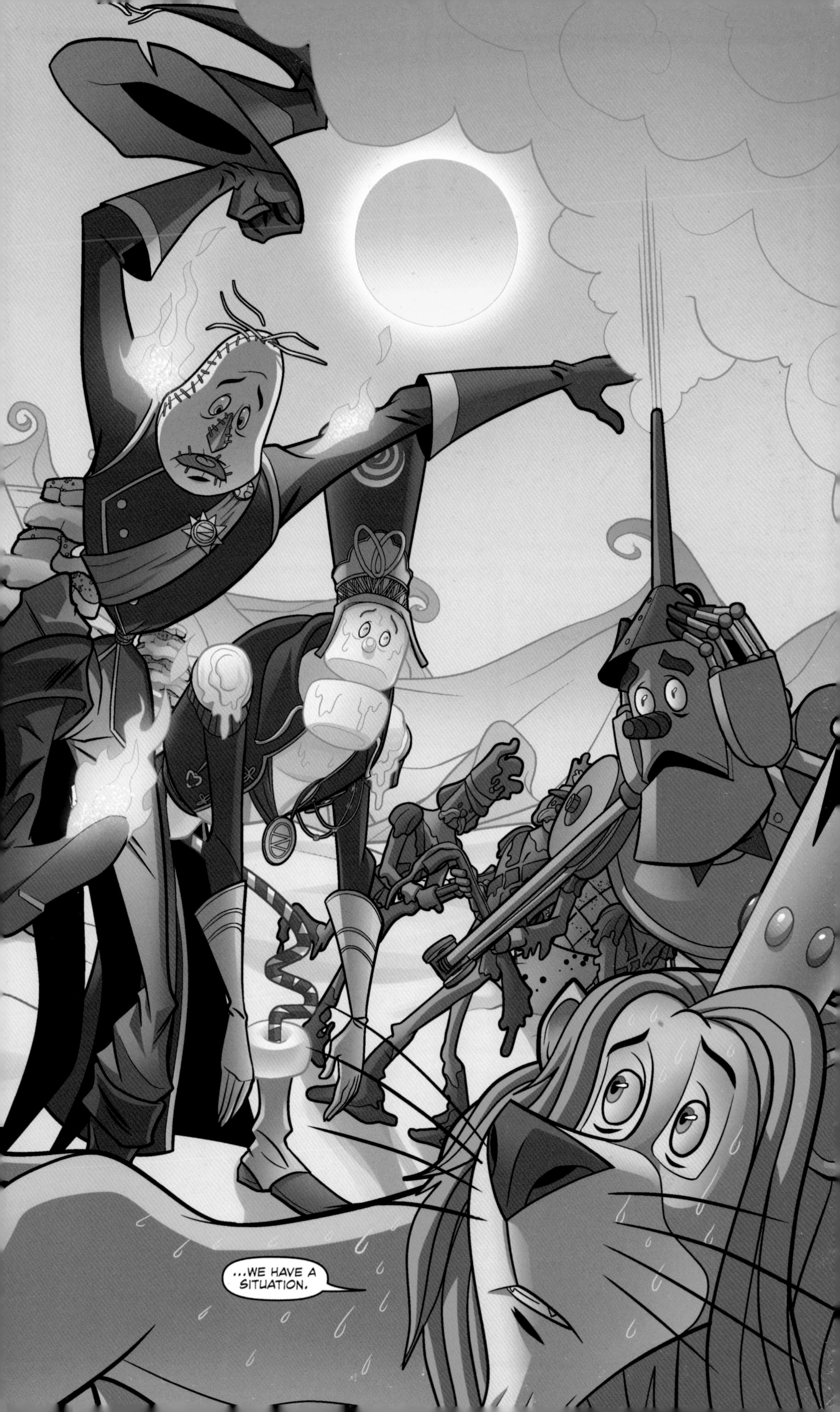
...WE HAVE A SITUATION.

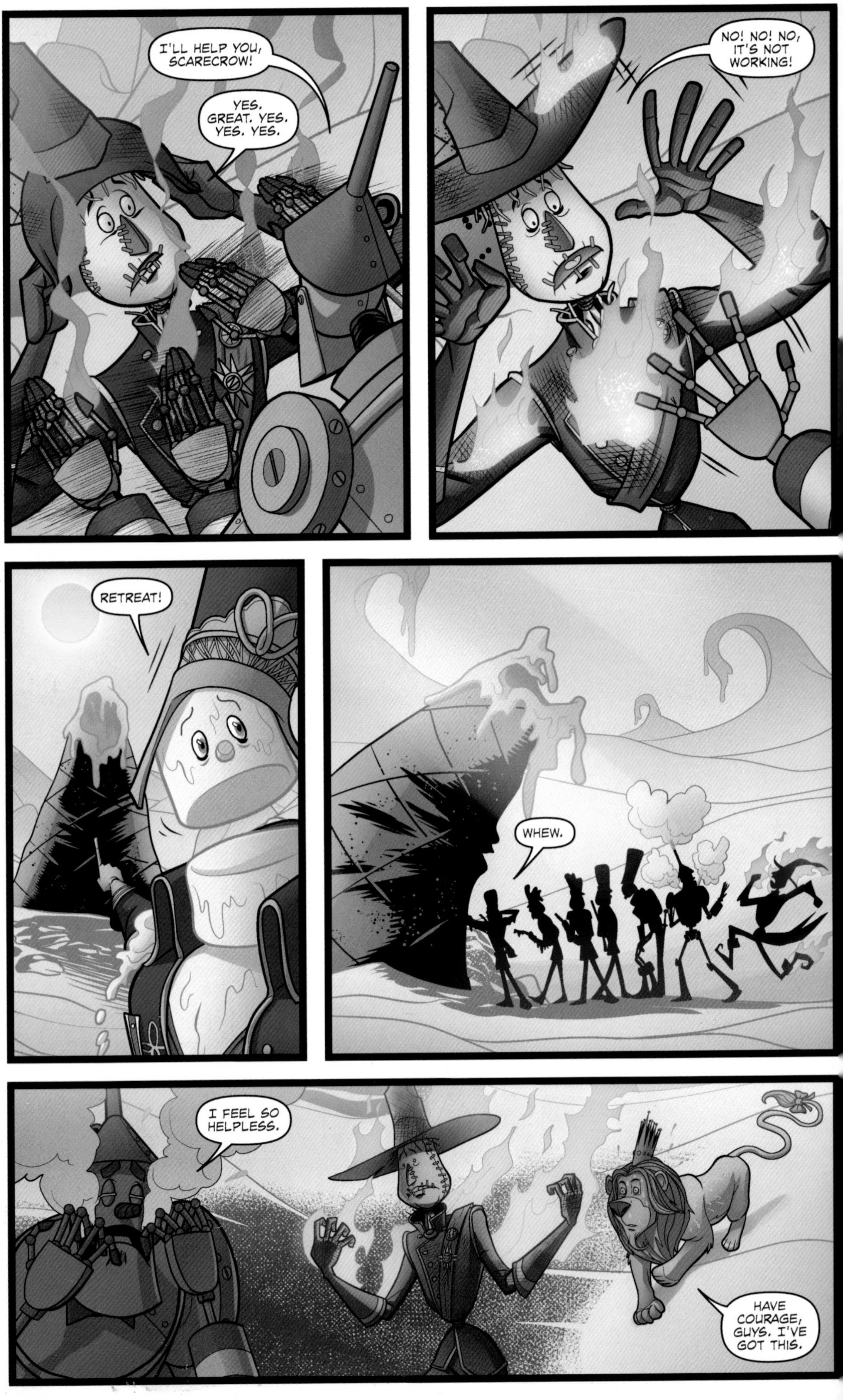
I'LL HELP YOU, SCARECROW!
YES. GREAT. YES. YES. YES.
NO! NO! NO, IT'S NOT WORKING!
RETREAT!
WHEW.
I FEEL SO HELPLESS.
HAVE COURAGE, GUYS. I'VE GOT THIS.

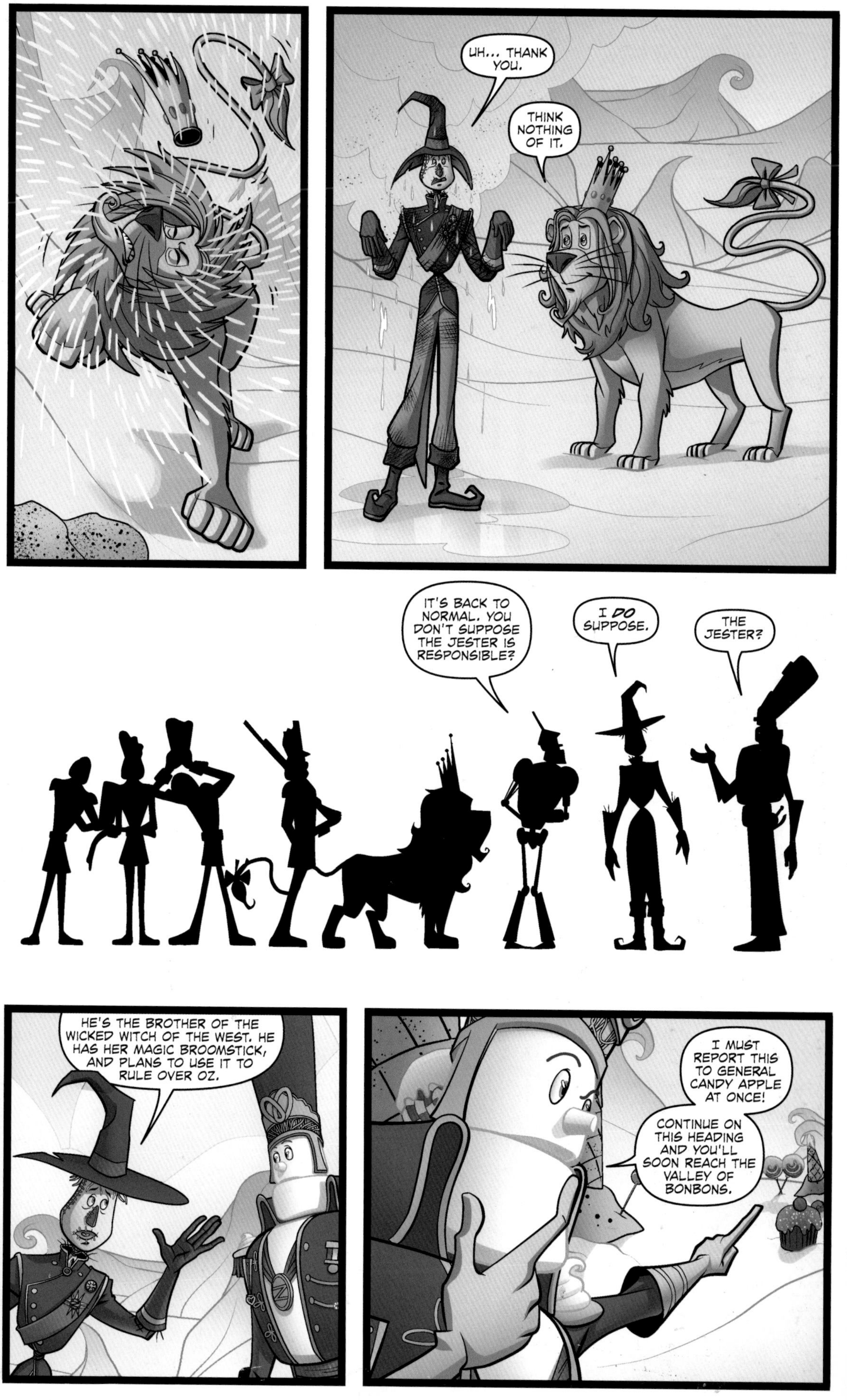
UH... THANK YOU.
THINK NOTHING OF IT.
IT'S BACK TO NORMAL. YOU DON'T SUPPOSE THE JESTER IS RESPONSIBLE?
I *DO* SUPPOSE.
THE JESTER?
HE'S THE BROTHER OF THE WICKED WITCH OF THE WEST. HE HAS HER MAGIC BROOMSTICK, AND PLANS TO USE IT TO RULE OVER OZ.
I MUST REPORT THIS TO GENERAL CANDY APPLE AT ONCE!
CONTINUE ON THIS HEADING AND YOU'LL SOON REACH THE VALLEY OF BONBONS.

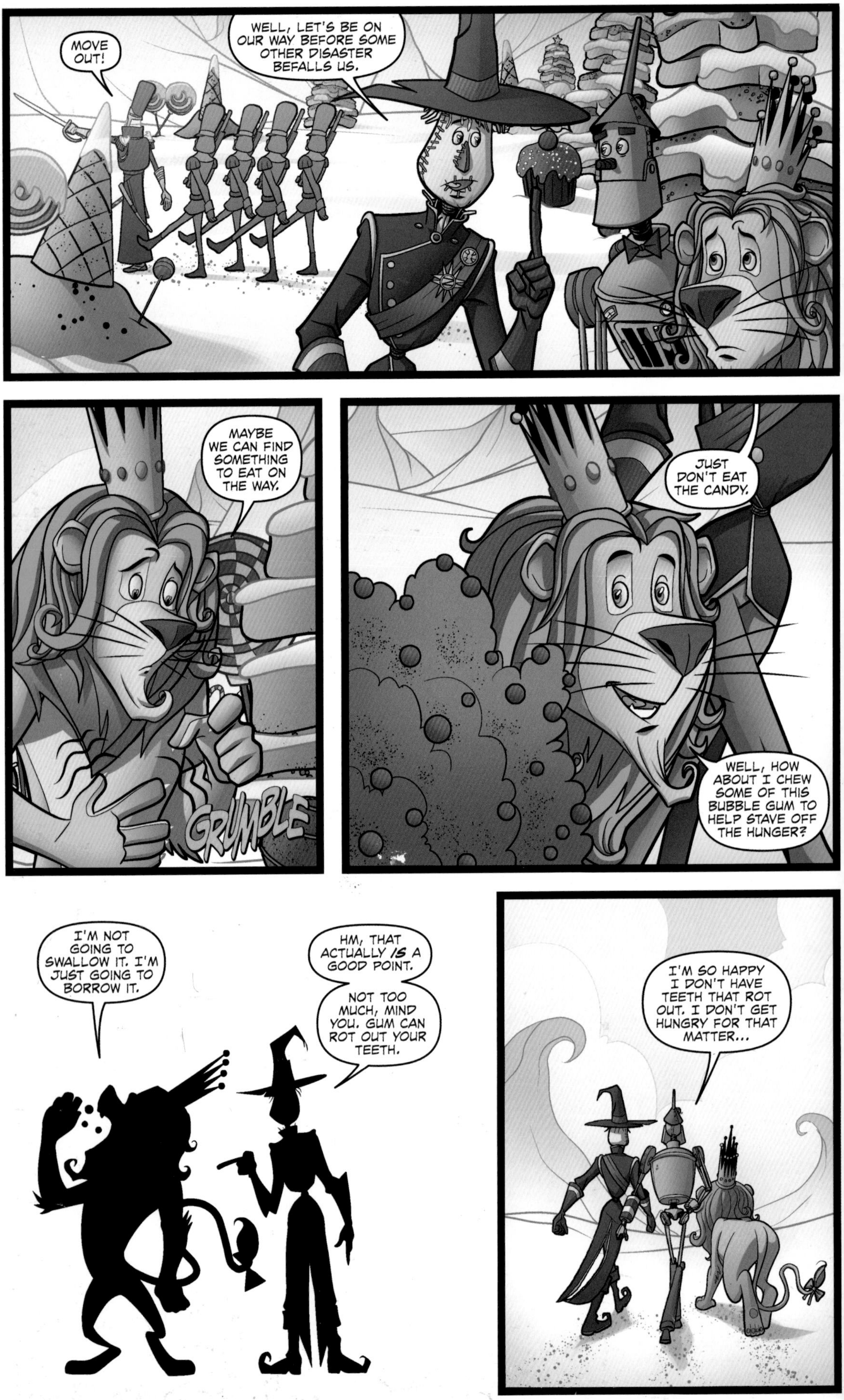
MOVE OUT!
WELL, LET'S BE ON OUR WAY BEFORE SOME OTHER DISASTER BEFALLS US.
MAYBE WE CAN FIND SOMETHING TO EAT ON THE WAY.
GRUMBLE
JUST DON'T EAT THE CANDY.
WELL, HOW ABOUT I CHEW SOME OF THIS BUBBLE GUM TO HELP STAVE OFF THE HUNGER?
HM, THAT ACTUALLY *IS* A GOOD POINT.
NOT TOO MUCH, MIND YOU. GUM CAN ROT OUT YOUR TEETH.
I'M NOT GOING TO SWALLOW IT. I'M JUST GOING TO BORROW IT.
I'M SO HAPPY I DON'T HAVE TEETH THAT ROT OUT. I DON'T GET HUNGRY FOR THAT MATTER...

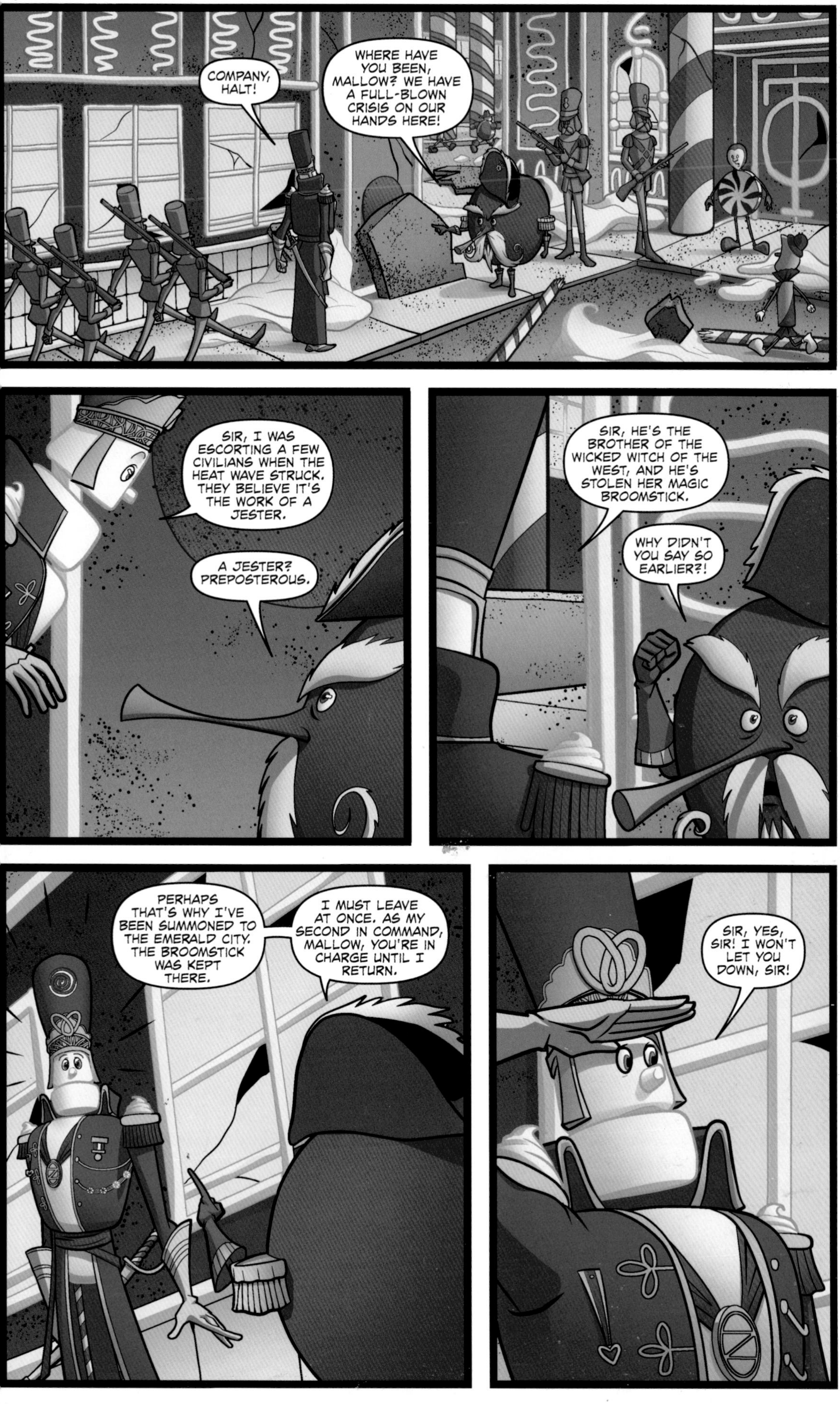
COMPANY, HALT!
WHERE HAVE YOU BEEN, MALLOW? WE HAVE A FULL-BLOWN CRISIS ON OUR HANDS HERE!
SIR, I WAS ESCORTING A FEW CIVILIANS WHEN THE HEAT WAVE STRUCK. THEY BELIEVE IT'S THE WORK OF A JESTER.
A JESTER? PREPOSTEROUS.
SIR, HE'S THE BROTHER OF THE WICKED WITCH OF THE WEST, AND HE'S STOLEN HER MAGIC BROOMSTICK.
WHY DIDN'T YOU SAY SO EARLIER?!
PERHAPS THAT'S WHY I'VE BEEN SUMMONED TO THE EMERALD CITY. THE BROOMSTICK WAS KEPT THERE.
I MUST LEAVE AT ONCE. AS MY SECOND IN COMMAND, MALLOW, YOU'RE IN CHARGE UNTIL I RETURN.
SIR, YES, SIR! I WON'T LET YOU DOWN, SIR!

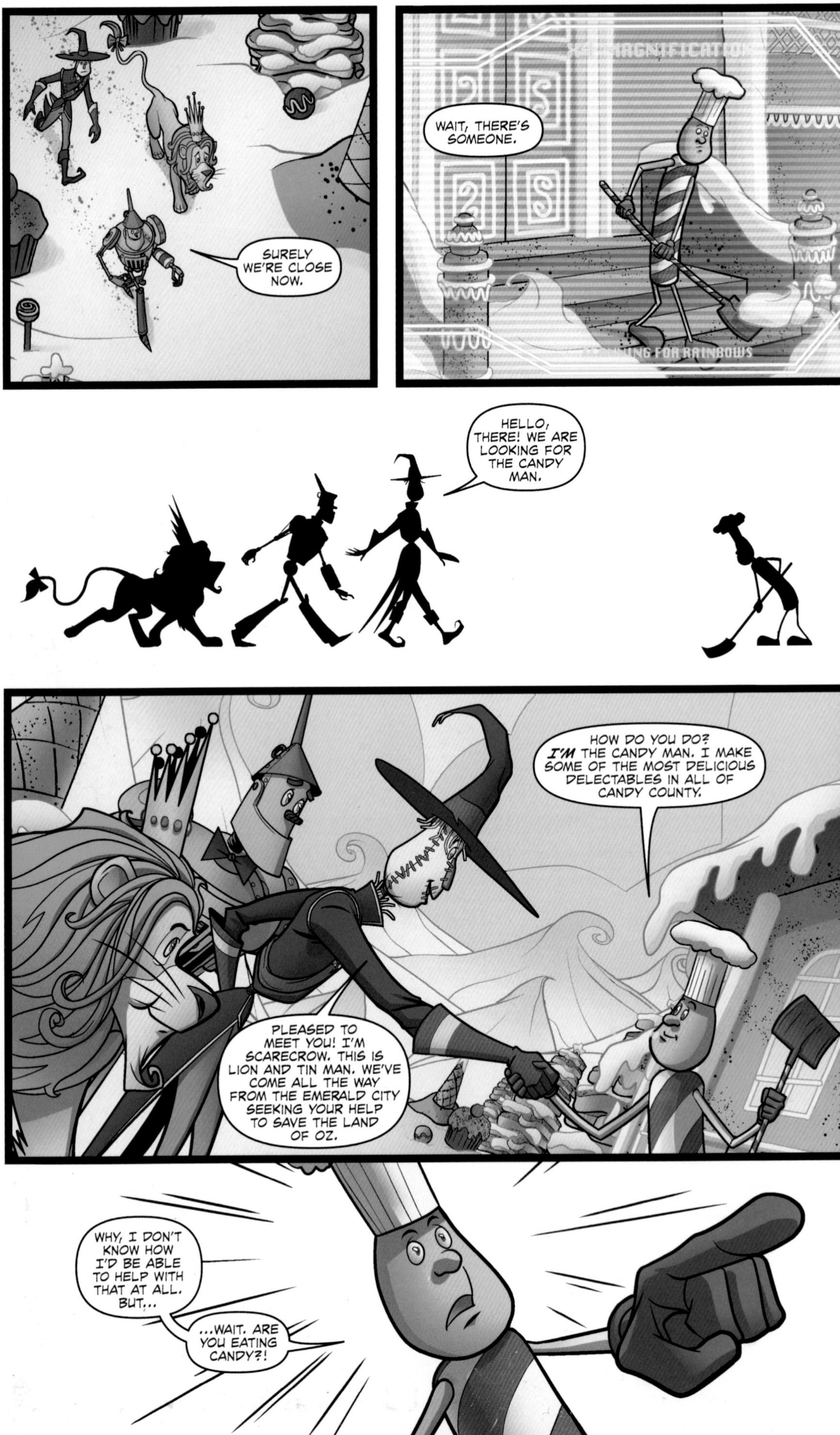
SURELY WE'RE CLOSE NOW.
WAIT, THERE'S SOMEONE.
HELLO, THERE! WE ARE LOOKING FOR THE CANDY MAN.
HOW DO YOU DO? *I'M* THE CANDY MAN. I MAKE SOME OF THE MOST DELICIOUS DELECTABLES IN ALL OF CANDY COUNTY.
PLEASED TO MEET YOU! I'M SCARECROW. THIS IS LION AND TIN MAN. WE'VE COME ALL THE WAY FROM THE EMERALD CITY SEEKING YOUR HELP TO SAVE THE LAND OF OZ.
WHY, I DON'T KNOW HOW I'D BE ABLE TO HELP WITH THAT AT ALL. BUT,...
...WAIT. ARE YOU EATING CANDY?!

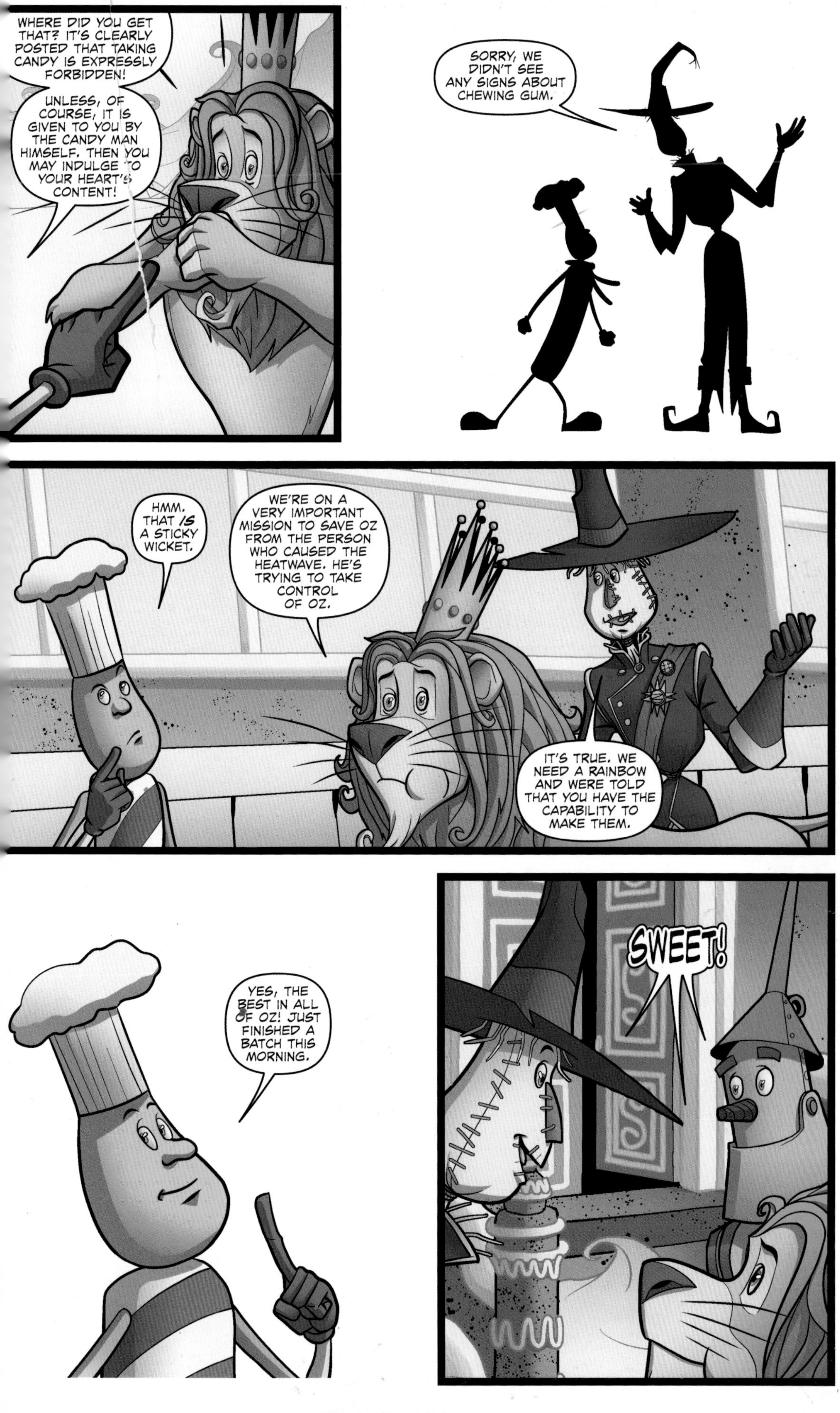
WHERE DID YOU GET THAT? IT'S CLEARLY POSTED THAT TAKING CANDY IS EXPRESSLY FORBIDDEN!
UNLESS, OF COURSE, IT IS GIVEN TO YOU BY THE CANDY MAN HIMSELF. THEN YOU MAY INDULGE TO YOUR HEART'S CONTENT!
SORRY, WE DIDN'T SEE ANY SIGNS ABOUT CHEWING GUM.
HMM. THAT *IS* A STICKY WICKET.
WE'RE ON A VERY IMPORTANT MISSION TO SAVE OZ FROM THE PERSON WHO CAUSED THE HEATWAVE. HE'S TRYING TO TAKE CONTROL OF OZ.
IT'S TRUE. WE NEED A RAINBOW AND WERE TOLD THAT YOU HAVE THE CAPABILITY TO MAKE THEM.
YES, THE BEST IN ALL OF OZ! JUST FINISHED A BATCH THIS MORNING.
SWEET!

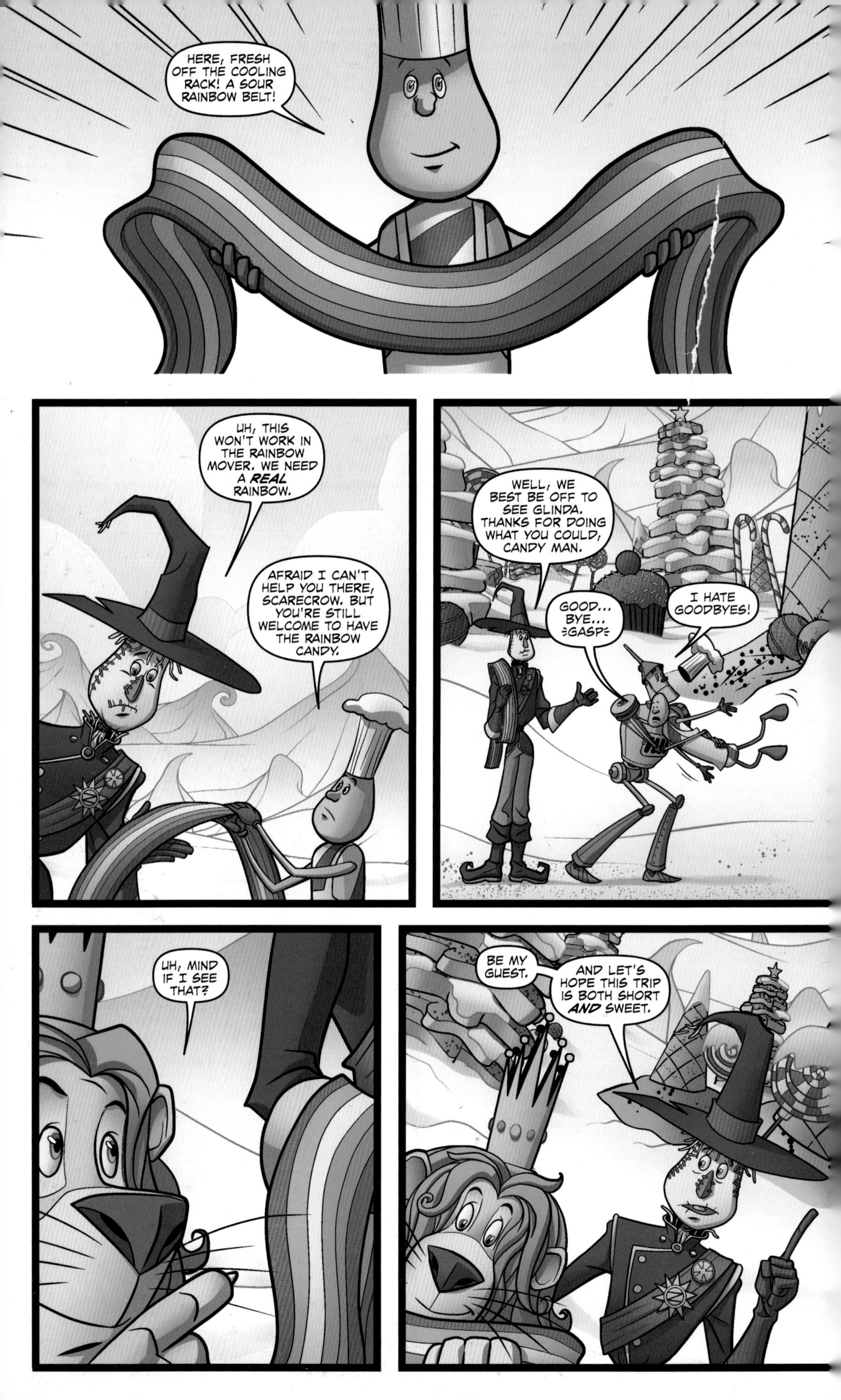

HERE, FRESH OFF THE COOLING RACK! A SOUR RAINBOW BELT!
UH, THIS WON'T WORK IN THE RAINBOW MOVER. WE NEED A *REAL* RAINBOW.
AFRAID I CAN'T HELP YOU THERE, SCARECROW. BUT YOU'RE STILL WELCOME TO HAVE THE RAINBOW CANDY.
WELL, WE BEST BE OFF TO SEE GLINDA. THANKS FOR DOING WHAT YOU COULD, CANDY MAN.
GOOD... BYE... GASP
I HATE GOODBYES!
UH, MIND IF I SEE THAT?
BE MY GUEST.
AND LET'S HOPE THIS TRIP IS BOTH SHORT *AND* SWEET.

FUDGE. POPS. LEMON DROPS.
WHAT THE--?!
FORM UP, MEN!
OH, FUDGE.

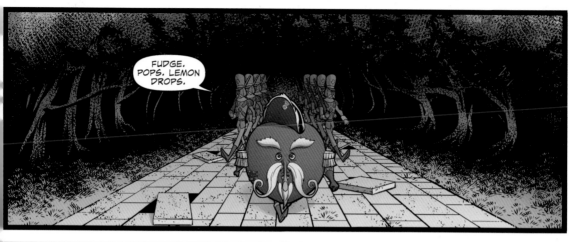

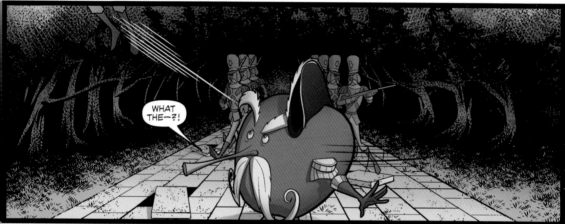

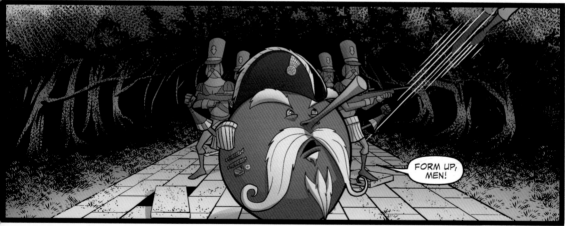

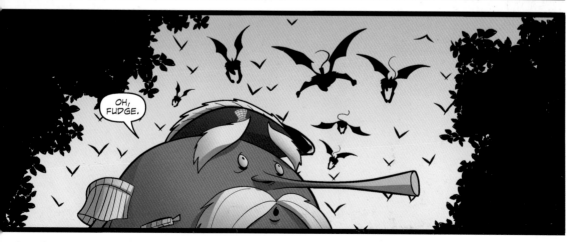

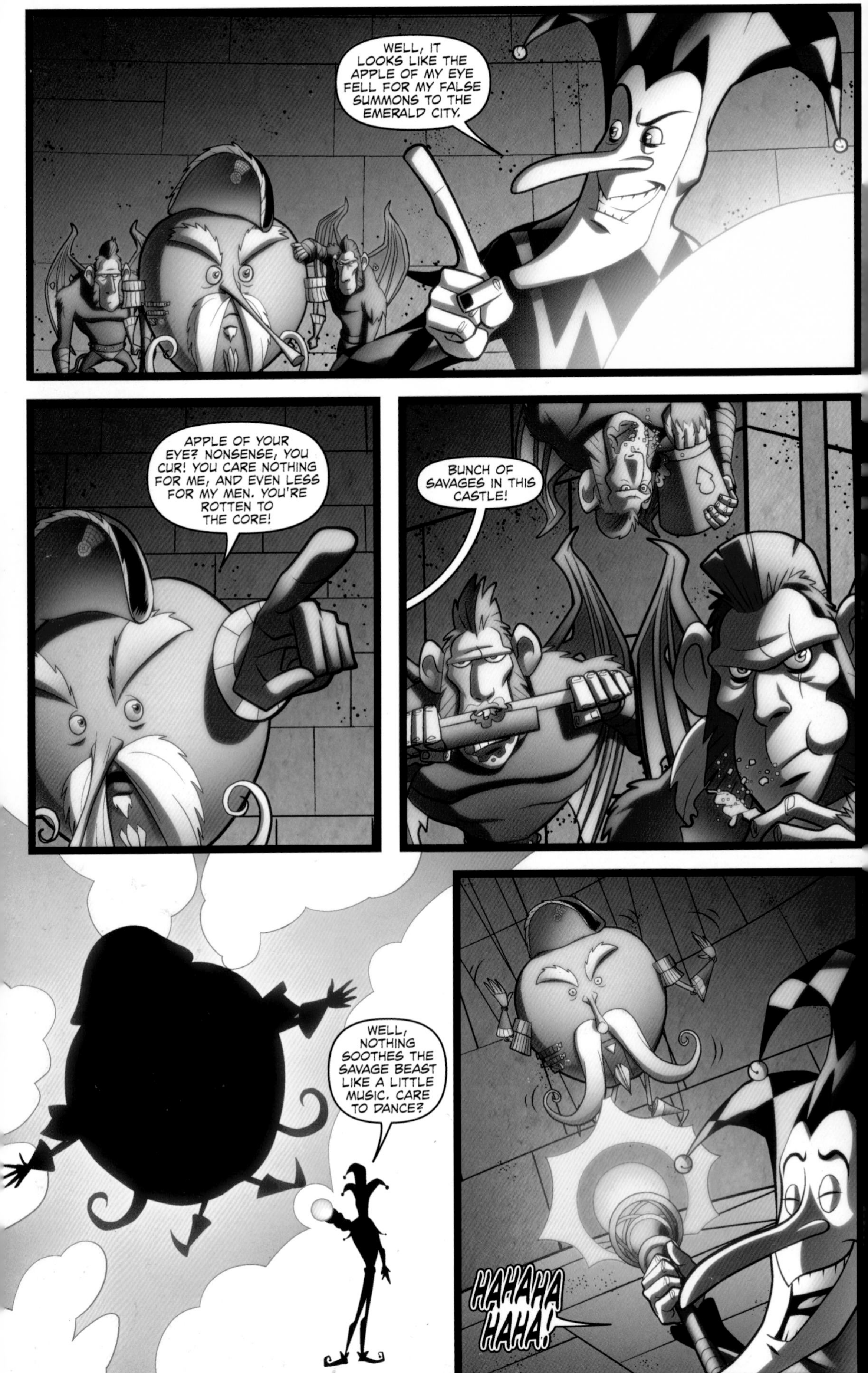
WELL, IT LOOKS LIKE THE APPLE OF MY EYE FELL FOR MY FALSE SUMMONS TO THE EMERALD CITY.
APPLE OF YOUR EYE? NONSENSE, YOU CUR! YOU CARE NOTHING FOR ME, AND EVEN LESS FOR MY MEN. YOU'RE ROTTEN TO THE CORE!
BUNCH OF SAVAGES IN THIS CASTLE!
WELL, NOTHING SOOTHES THE SAVAGE BEAST LIKE A LITTLE MUSIC. CARE TO DANCE?
HAHAHA HAHA!

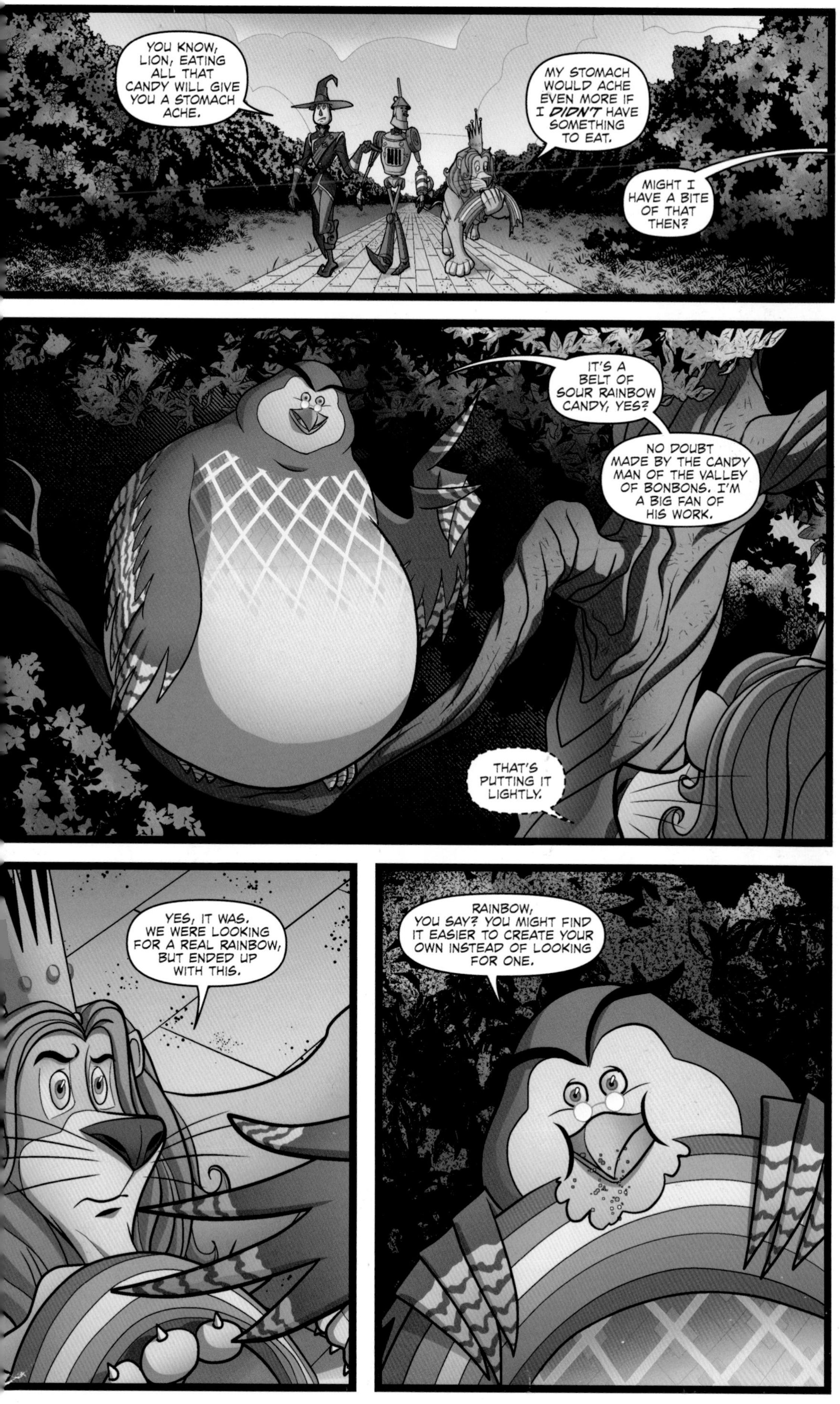
YOU KNOW, LION, EATING ALL THAT CANDY WILL GIVE YOU A STOMACH ACHE.
MY STOMACH WOULD ACHE EVEN MORE IF I *DIDN'T* HAVE SOMETHING TO EAT.
MIGHT I HAVE A BITE OF THAT THEN?
IT'S A BELT OF SOUR RAINBOW CANDY, YES?
NO DOUBT MADE BY THE CANDY MAN OF THE VALLEY OF BONBONS. I'M A BIG FAN OF HIS WORK.
THAT'S PUTTING IT LIGHTLY.
YES, IT WAS. WE WERE LOOKING FOR A REAL RAINBOW, BUT ENDED UP WITH THIS.
RAINBOW, YOU SAY? YOU MIGHT FIND IT EASIER TO CREATE YOUR OWN INSTEAD OF LOOKING FOR ONE.

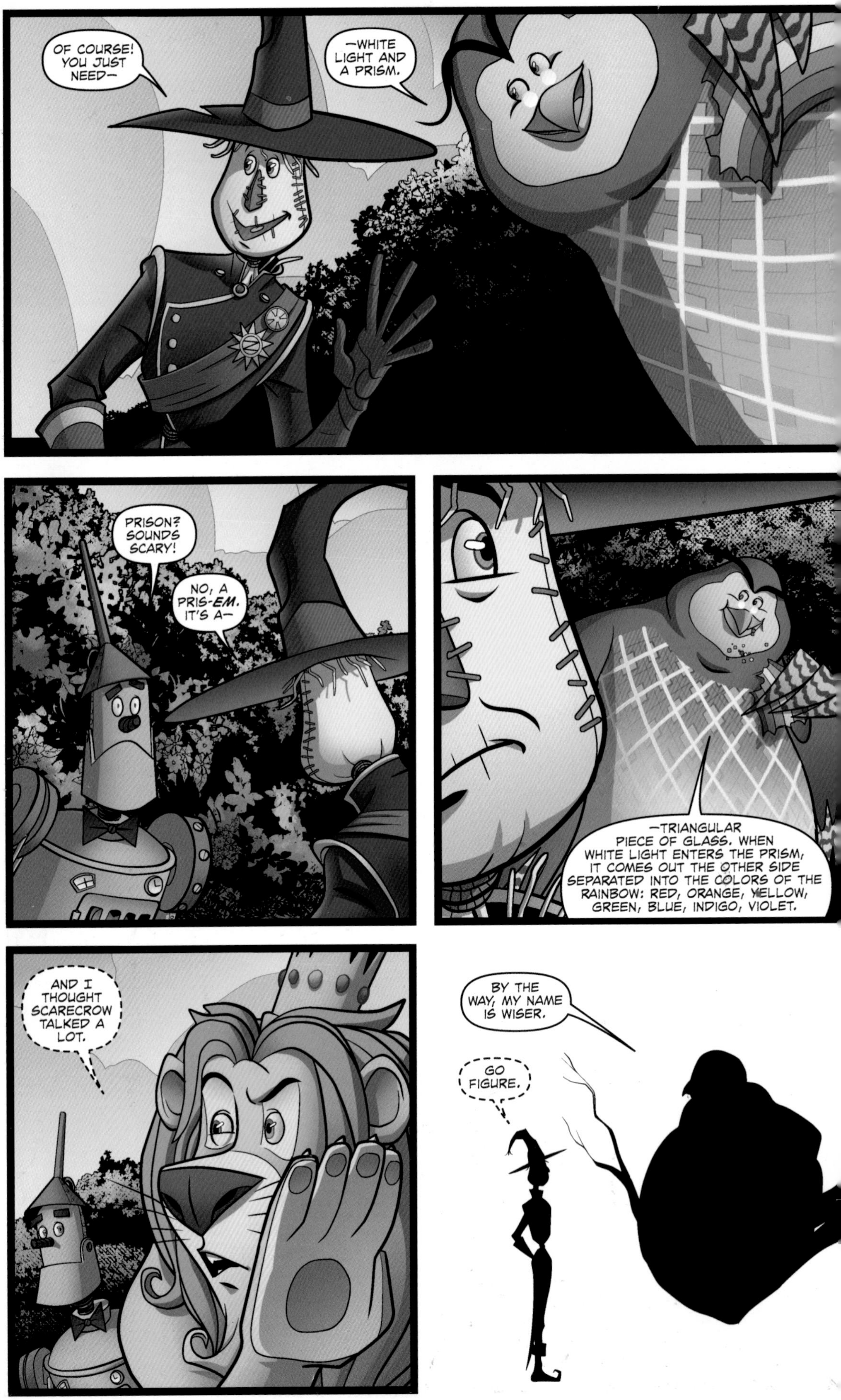
OF COURSE! YOU JUST NEED—
—WHITE LIGHT AND A PRISM.
PRISON? SOUNDS SCARY!
NO, A PRIS-*EM*. IT'S A—
—TRIANGULAR PIECE OF GLASS. WHEN WHITE LIGHT ENTERS THE PRISM, IT COMES OUT THE OTHER SIDE SEPARATED INTO THE COLORS OF THE RAINBOW: RED, ORANGE, YELLOW, GREEN, BLUE, INDIGO, VIOLET.
AND I THOUGHT SCARECROW TALKED A LOT.
BY THE WAY, MY NAME IS WISER.
GO FIGURE.

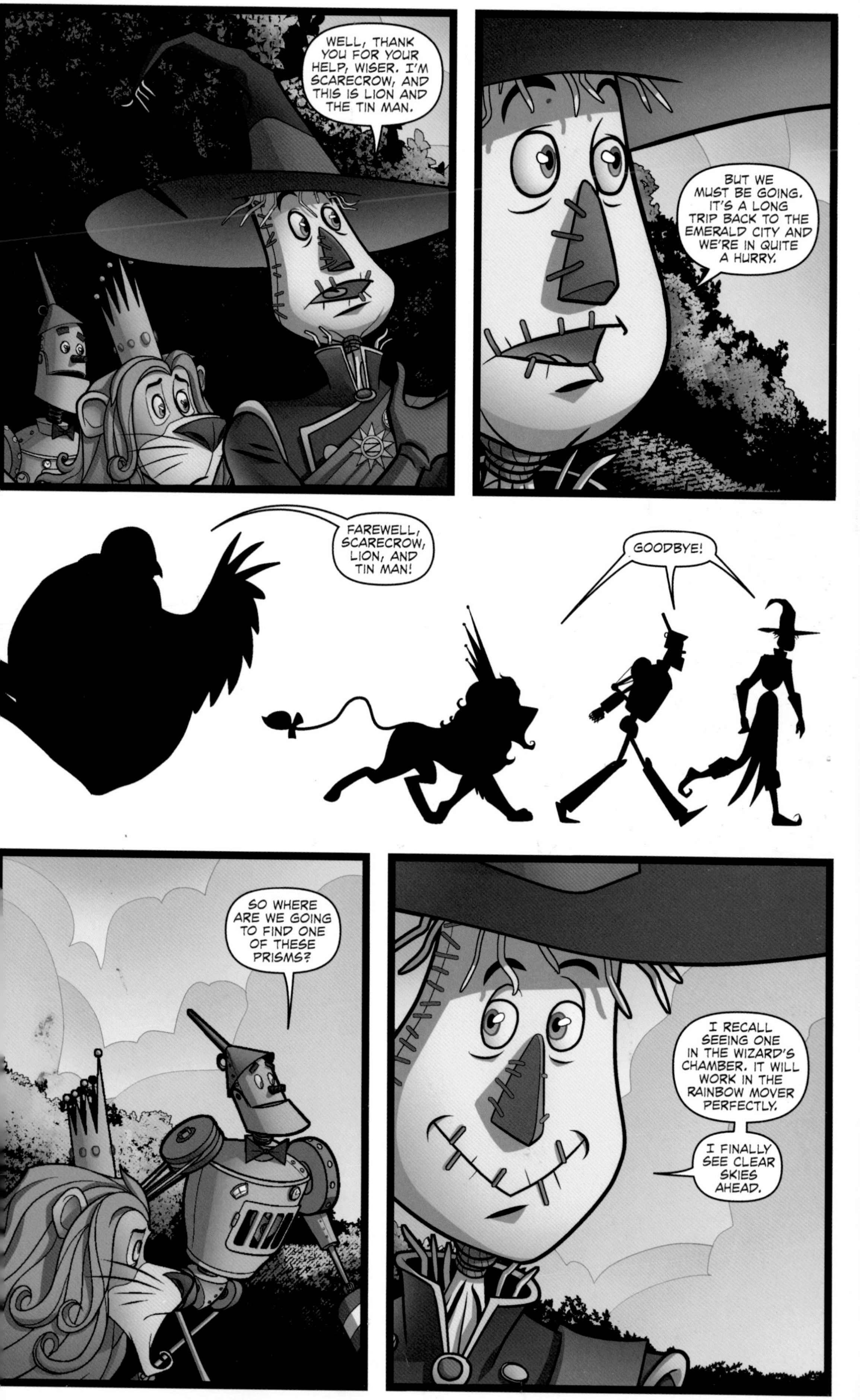
WELL, THANK YOU FOR YOUR HELP, WISER. I'M SCARECROW, AND THIS IS LION AND THE TIN MAN.
BUT WE MUST BE GOING. IT'S A LONG TRIP BACK TO THE EMERALD CITY AND WE'RE IN QUITE A HURRY.
FAREWELL, SCARECROW, LION, AND TIN MAN!
GOODBYE!
SO WHERE ARE WE GOING TO FIND ONE OF THESE PRISMS?
I RECALL SEEING ONE IN THE WIZARD'S CHAMBER. IT WILL WORK IN THE RAINBOW MOVER PERFECTLY.
I FINALLY SEE CLEAR SKIES AHEAD.

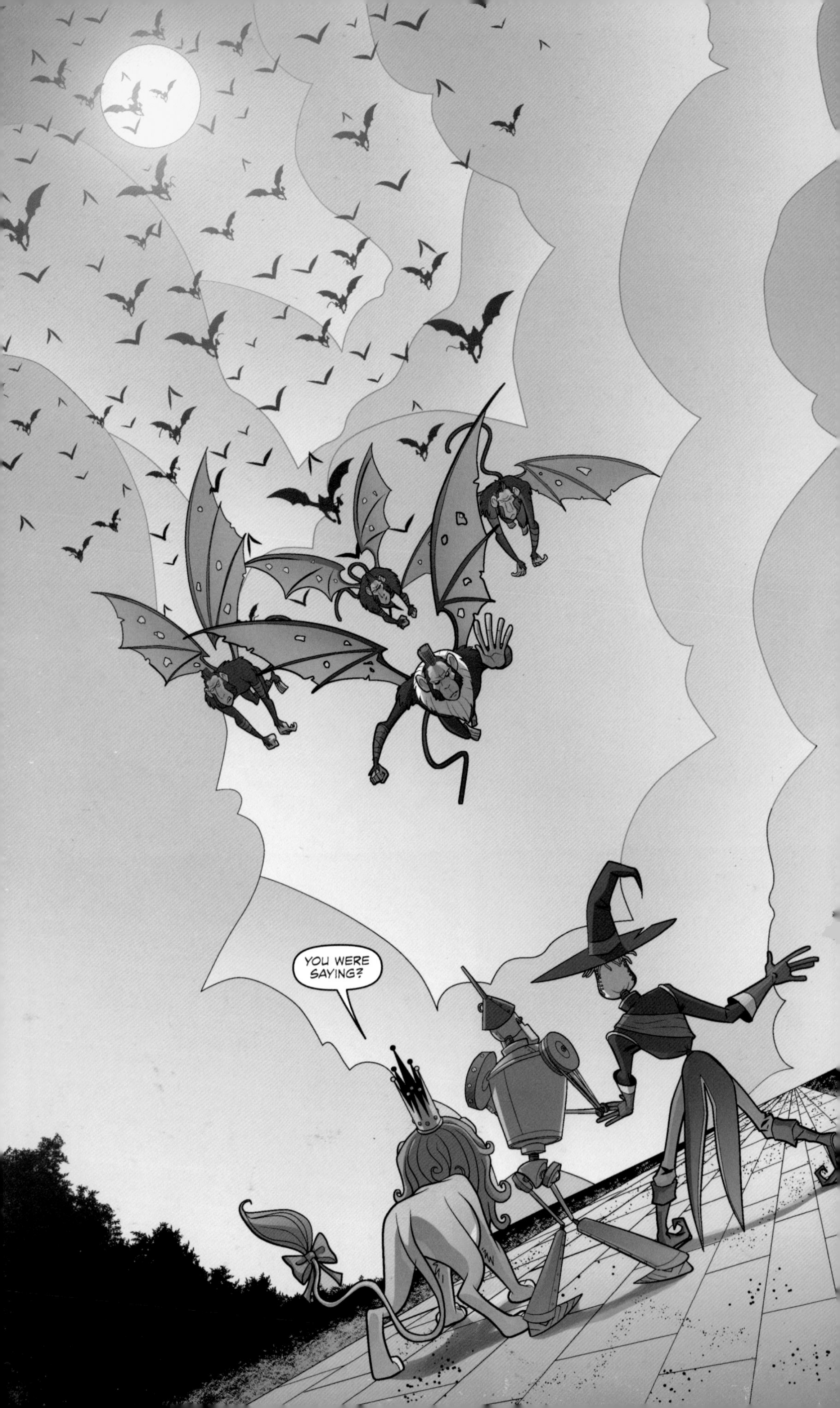
YOU WERE SAYING?

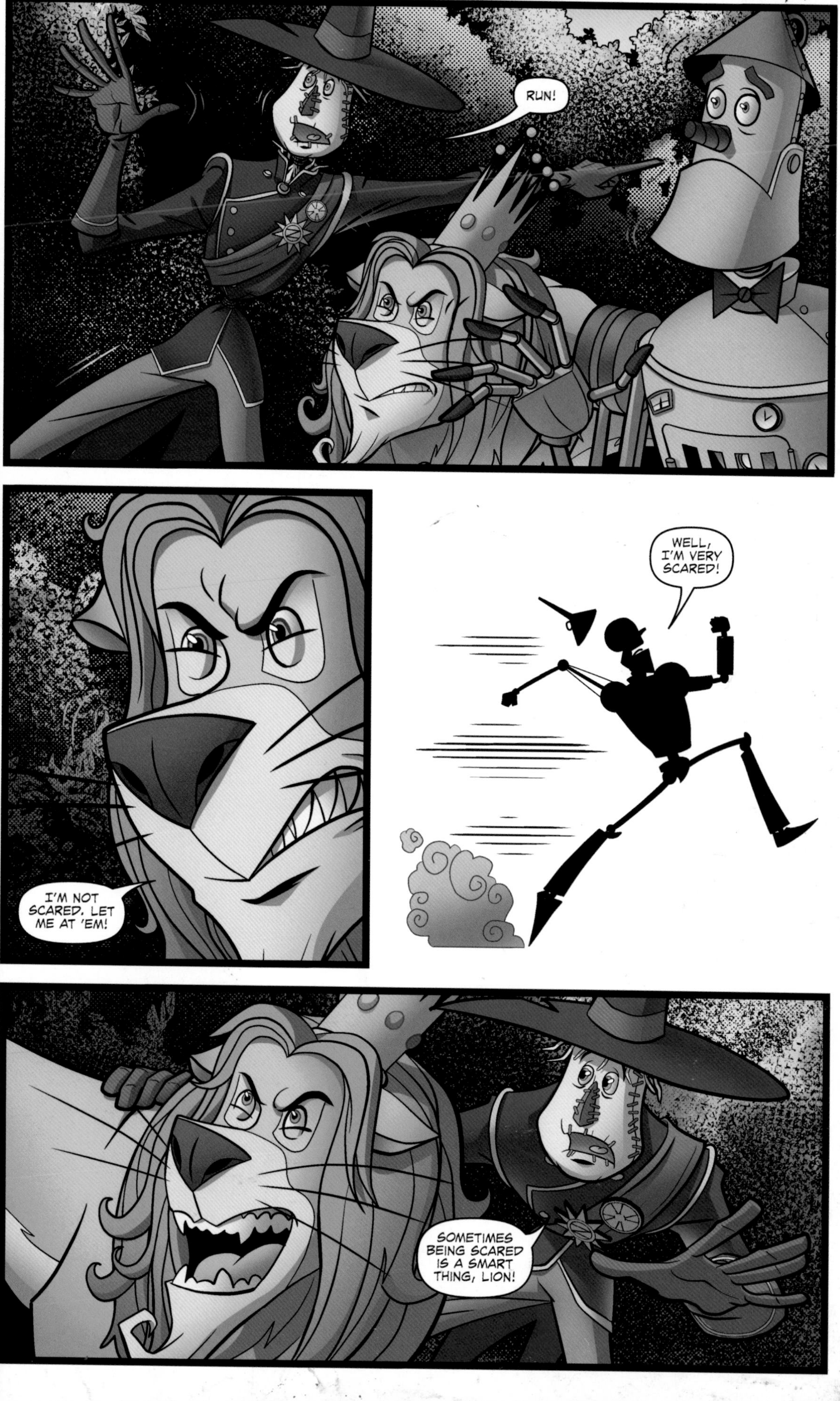
RUN!
I'M NOT SCARED. LET ME AT 'EM!
WELL, I'M VERY SCARED!
SOMETIMES BEING SCARED IS A SMART THING, LION!

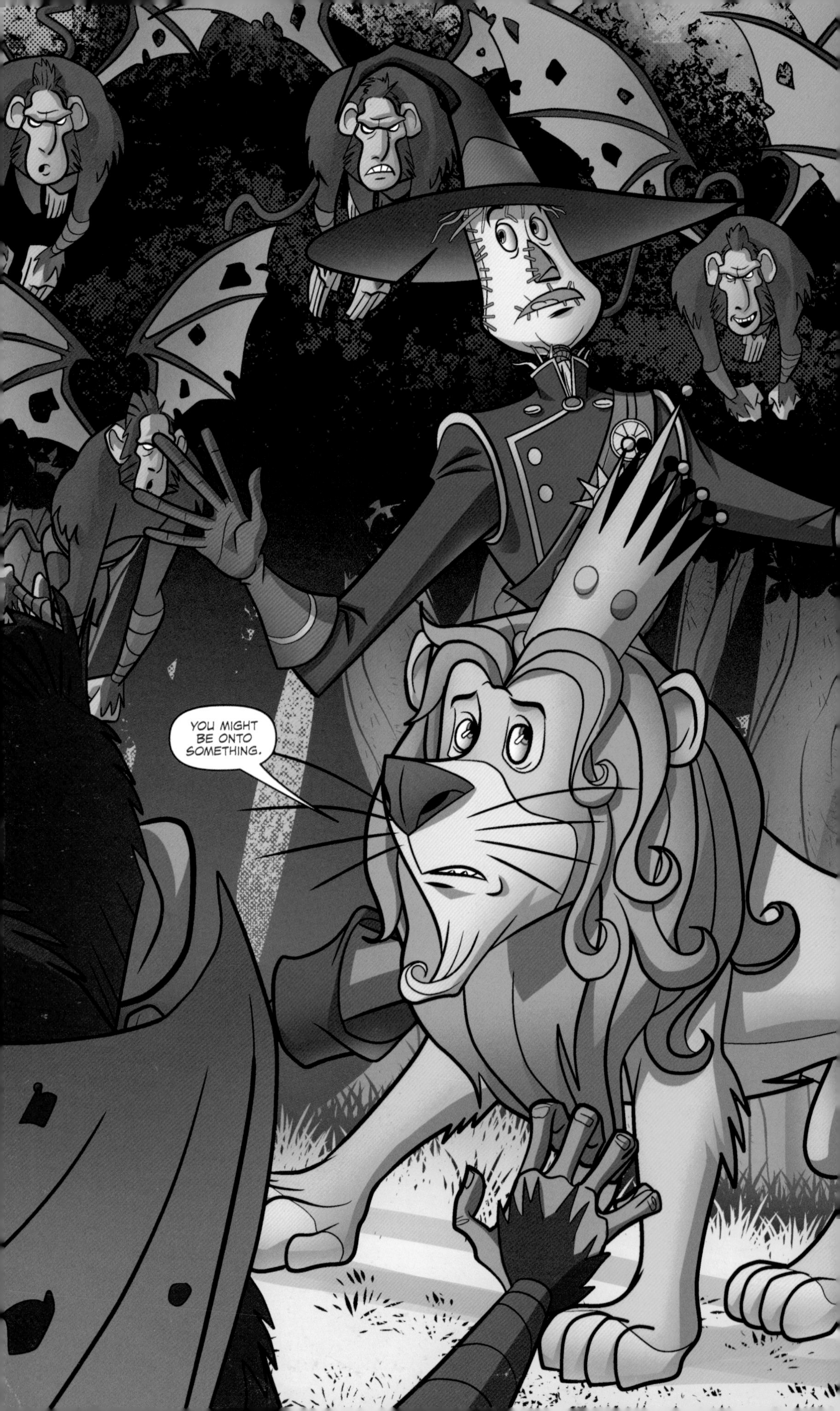
YOU MIGHT BE ONTO SOMETHING.

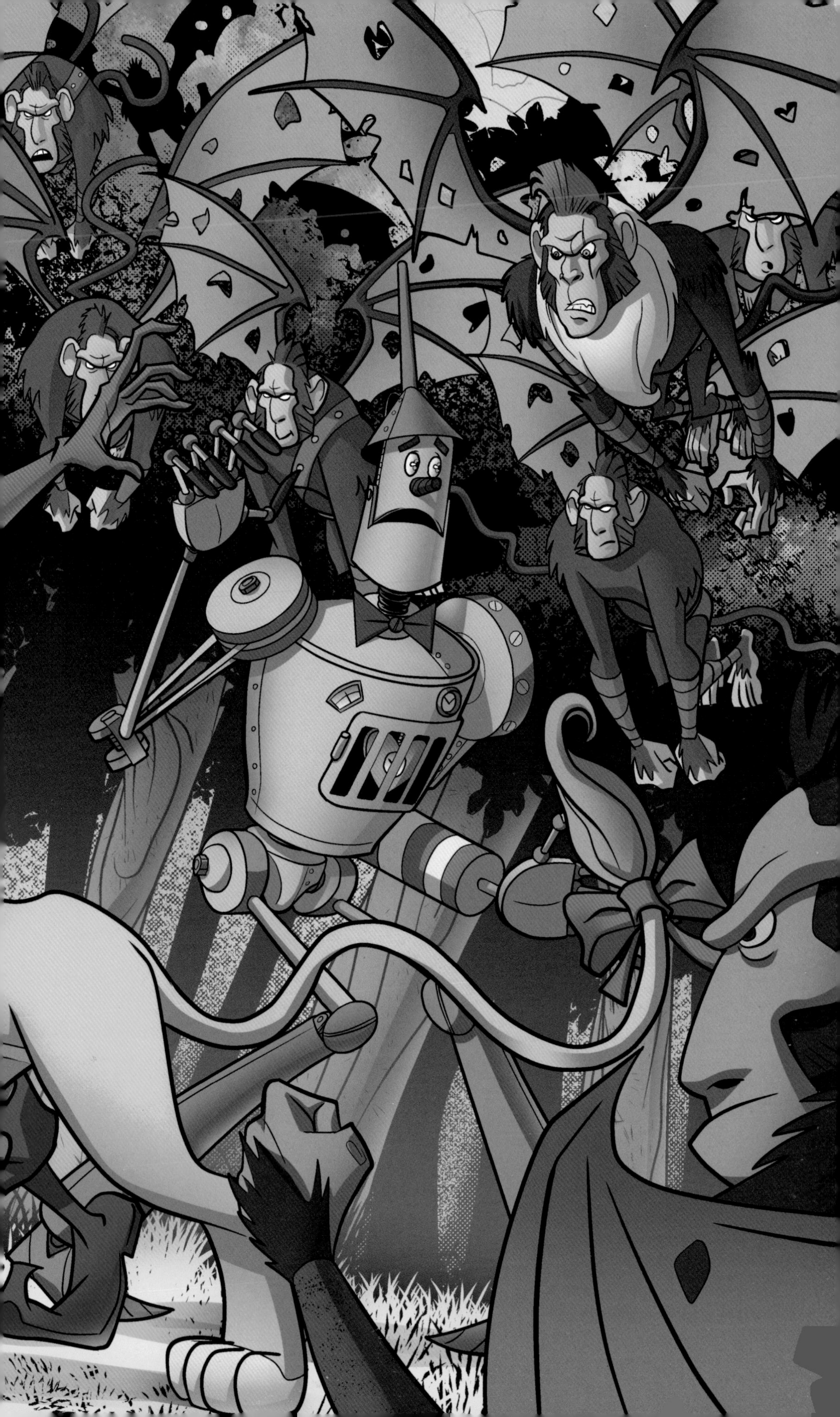

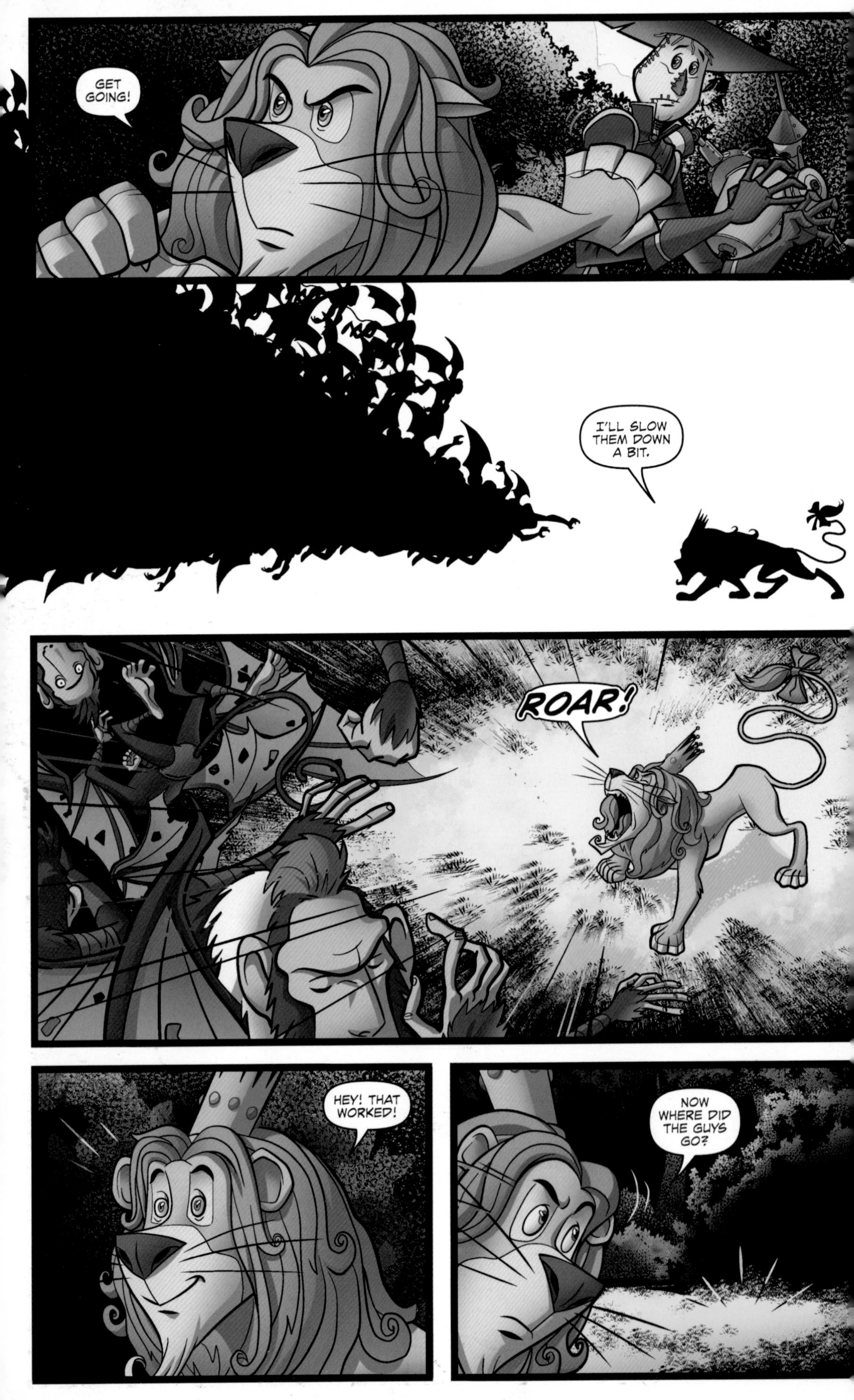
GET GOING!
I'LL SLOW THEM DOWN A BIT.
ROAR!
HEY! THAT WORKED!
NOW WHERE DID THE GUYS GO?

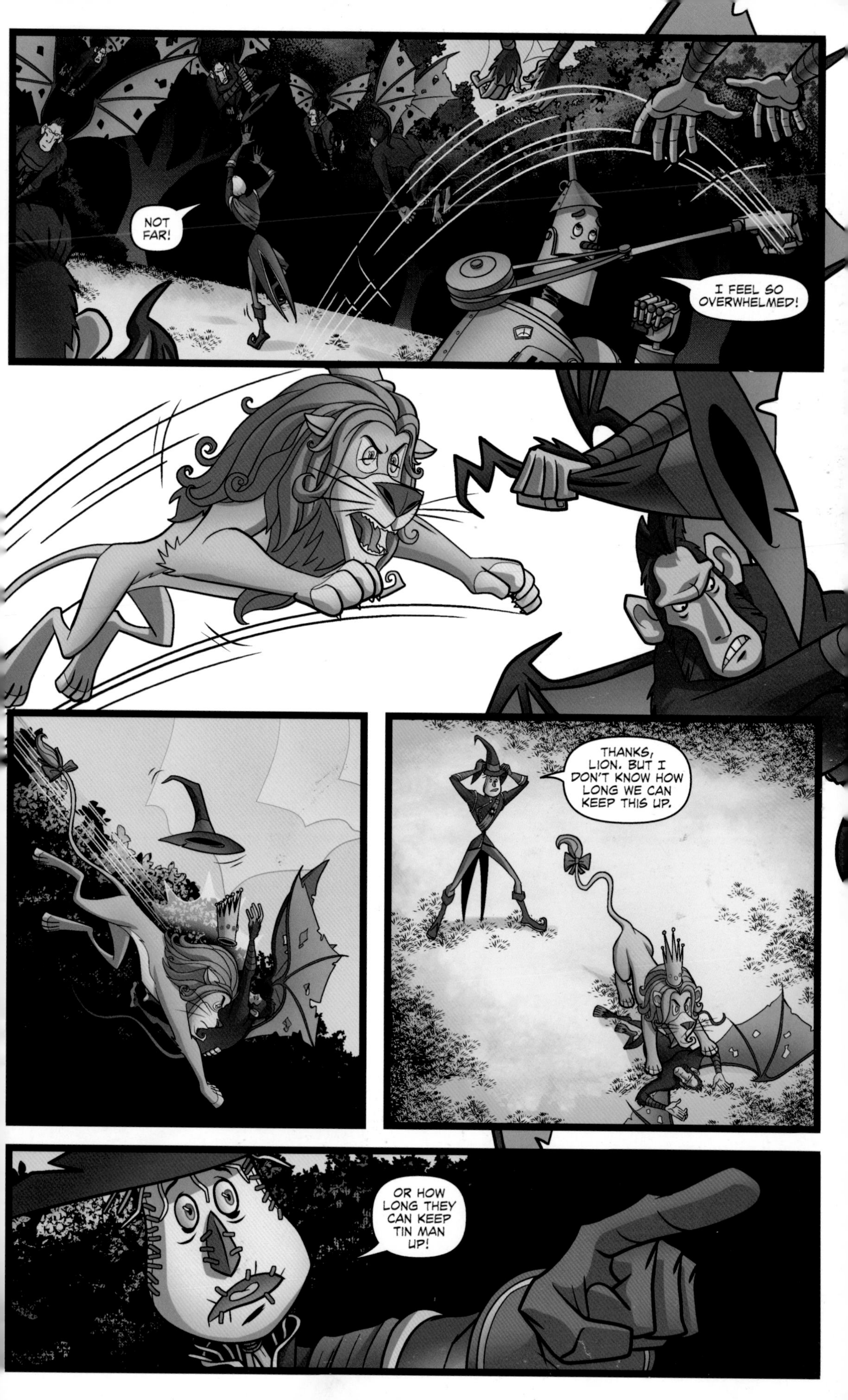
NOT FAR!
I FEEL SO OVERWHELMED!
THANKS, LION. BUT I DON'T KNOW HOW LONG WE CAN KEEP THIS UP.
OR HOW LONG THEY CAN KEEP TIN MAN UP!

LITTLE HELP, GUYS?!

THEY WON'T KEEP HIM UP LONG IF I HAVE ANYTHING TO DO WITH IT!

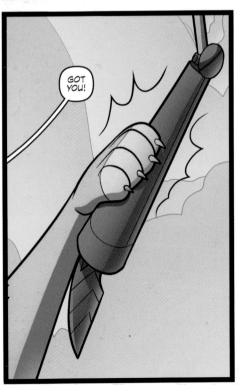

GOT YOU!

BUT WHO'S GOT *YOU*?!

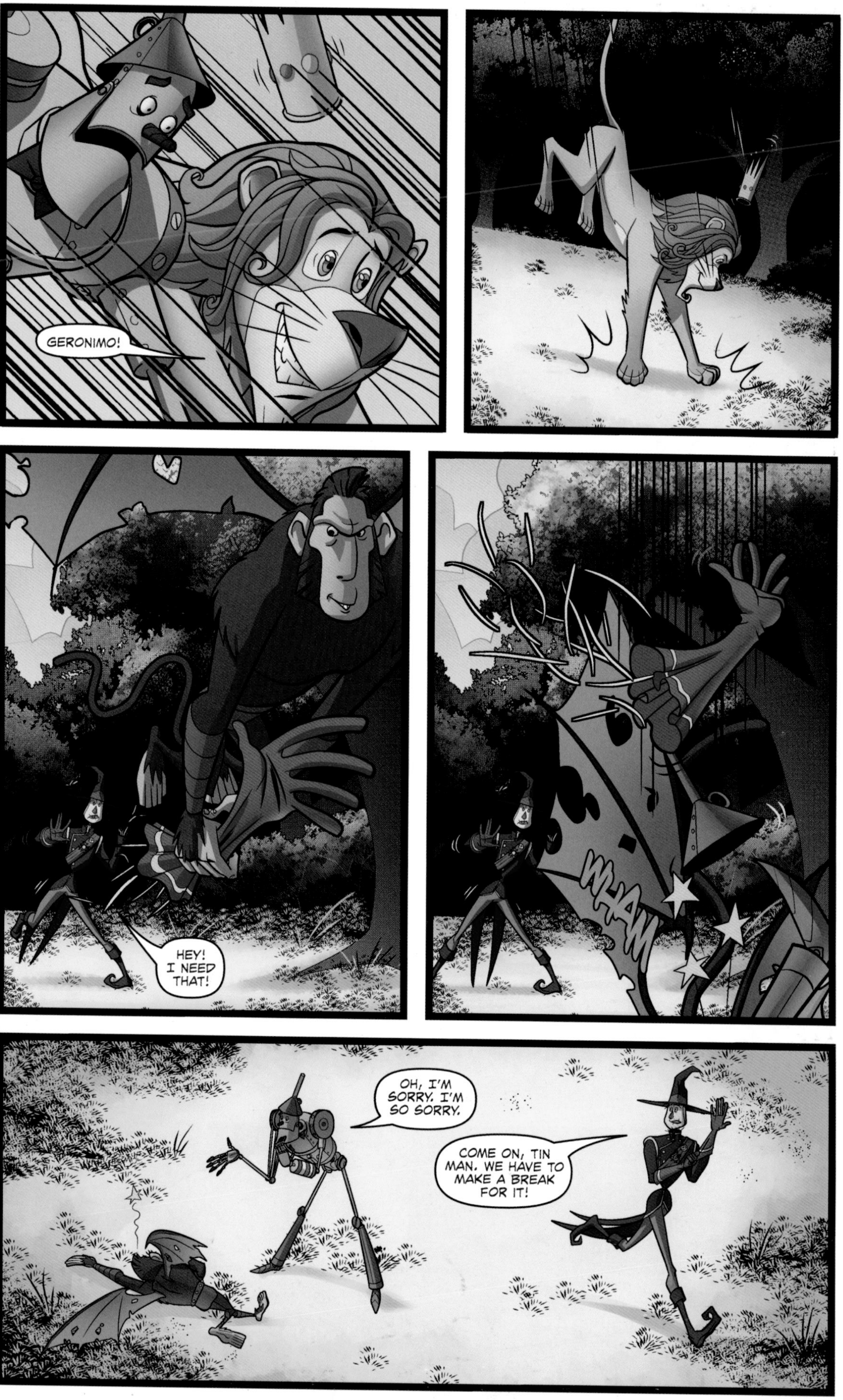
GERONIMO!
HEY! I NEED THAT!
WHAM
OH, I'M SORRY. I'M SO SORRY.
COME ON, TIN MAN. WE HAVE TO MAKE A BREAK FOR IT!

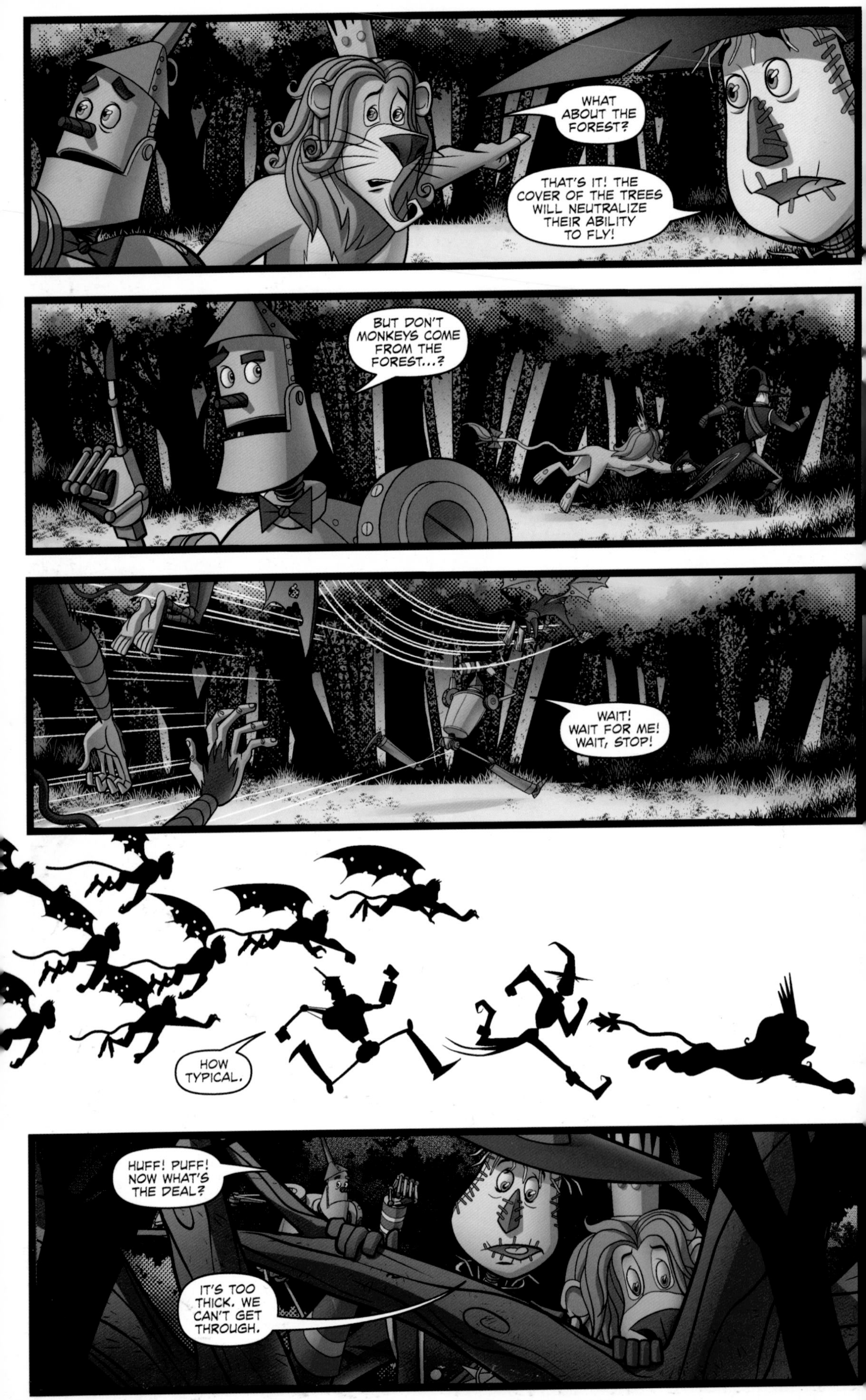
WHAT ABOUT THE FOREST?
THAT'S IT! THE COVER OF THE TREES WILL NEUTRALIZE THEIR ABILITY TO FLY!
BUT DON'T MONKEYS COME FROM THE FOREST...?
WAIT! WAIT FOR ME! WAIT, STOP!
HOW TYPICAL.
HUFF! PUFF! NOW WHAT'S THE DEAL?
IT'S TOO THICK. WE CAN'T GET THROUGH.

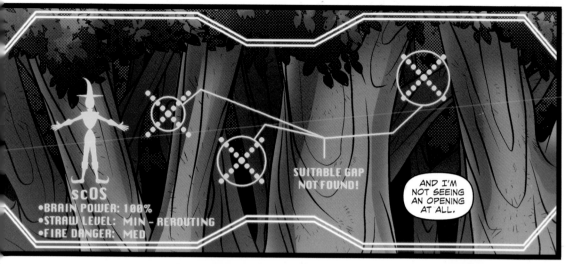

scOS
• BRAIN POWER: 100%
• STRAW LEVEL: MIN – REROUTING
• FIRE DANGER: MED

SUITABLE GAP NOT FOUND!

AND I'M NOT SEEING AN OPENING AT ALL.

THEN WE MAKE OUR FINAL STAND HERE.

DID YOU HAVE TO SAY FINAL?

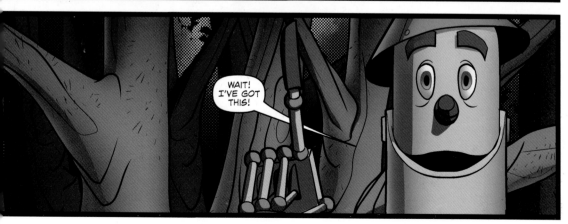

WAIT! I'VE GOT THIS!

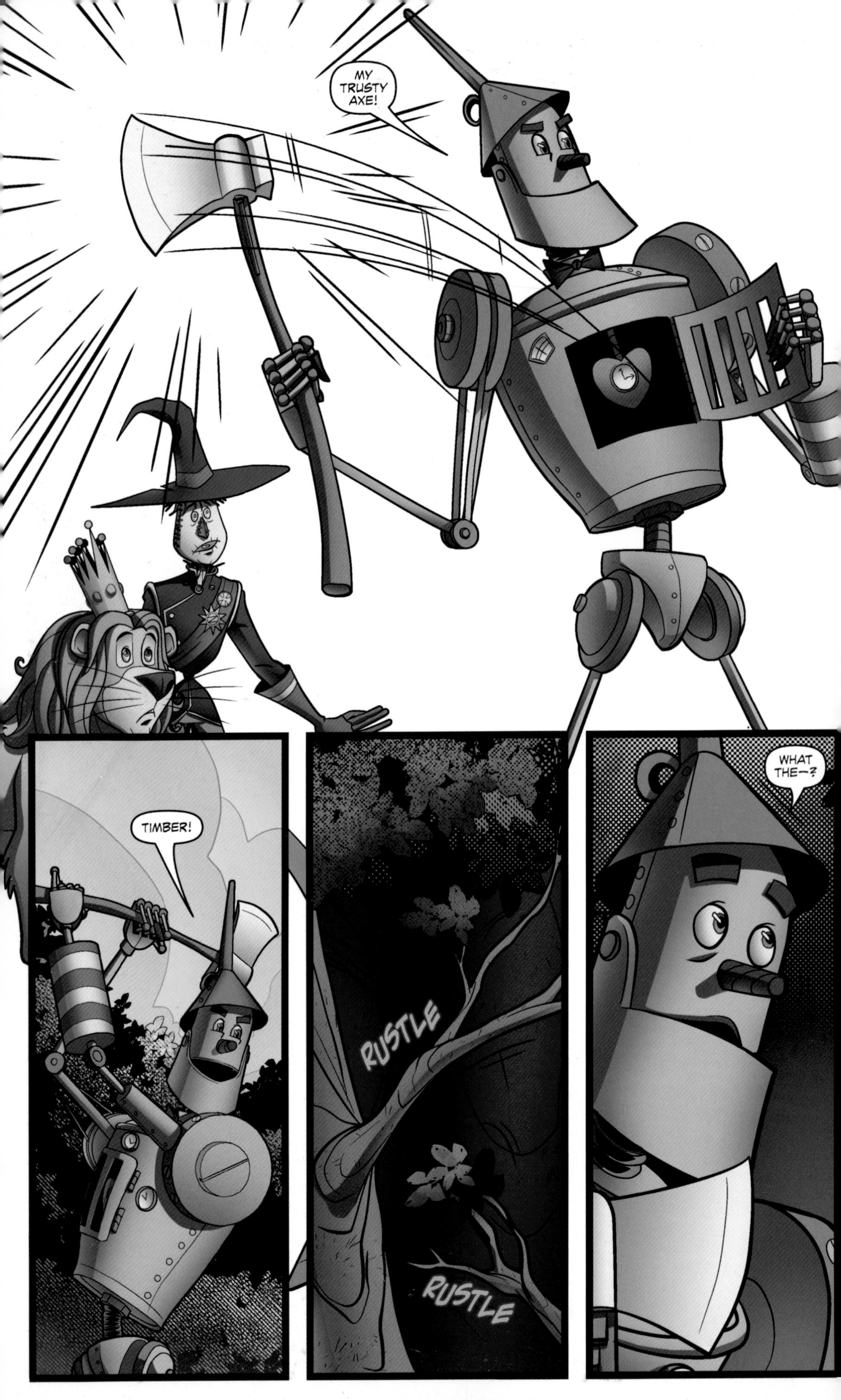
MY TRUSTY AXE!
TIMBER!
RUSTLE
RUSTLE
WHAT THE—?

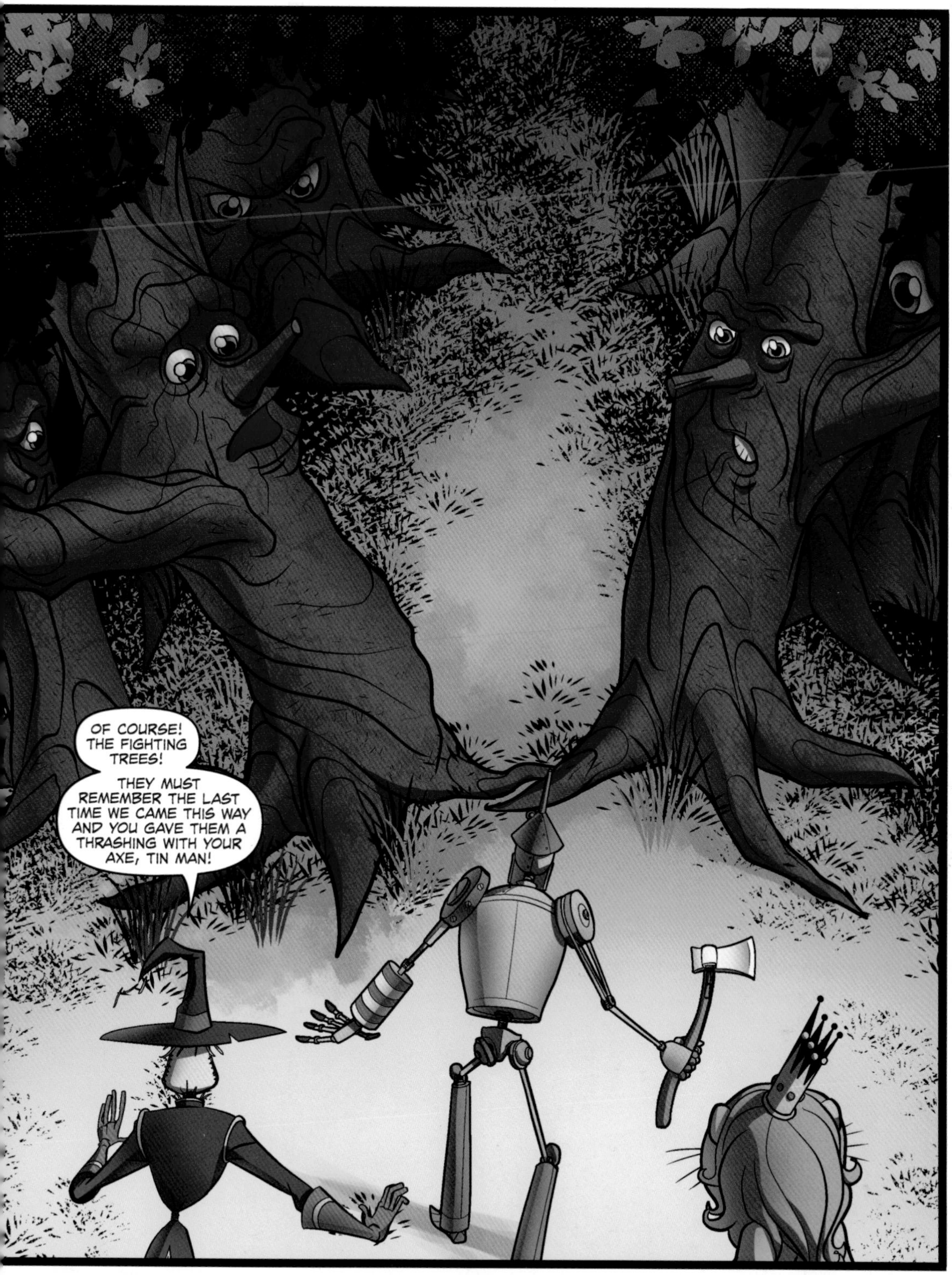
OF COURSE! THE FIGHTING TREES!
THEY MUST REMEMBER THE LAST TIME WE CAME THIS WAY AND YOU GAVE THEM A THRASHING WITH YOUR AXE, TIN MAN!

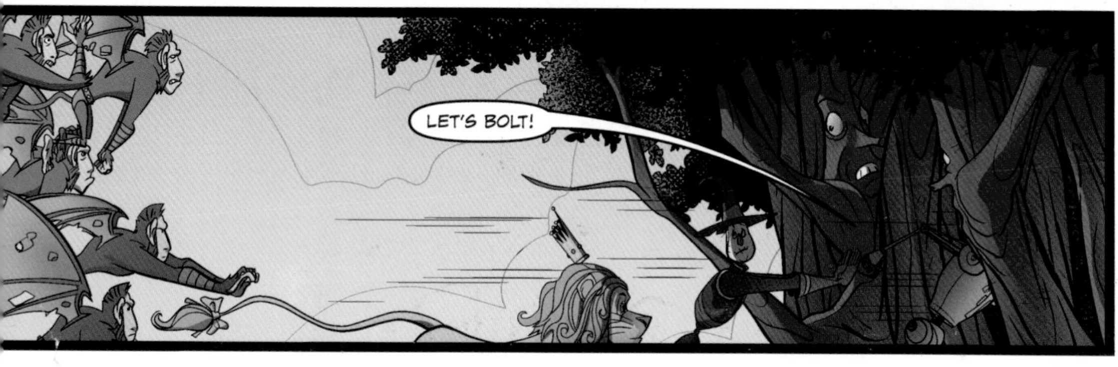
LET'S BOLT!

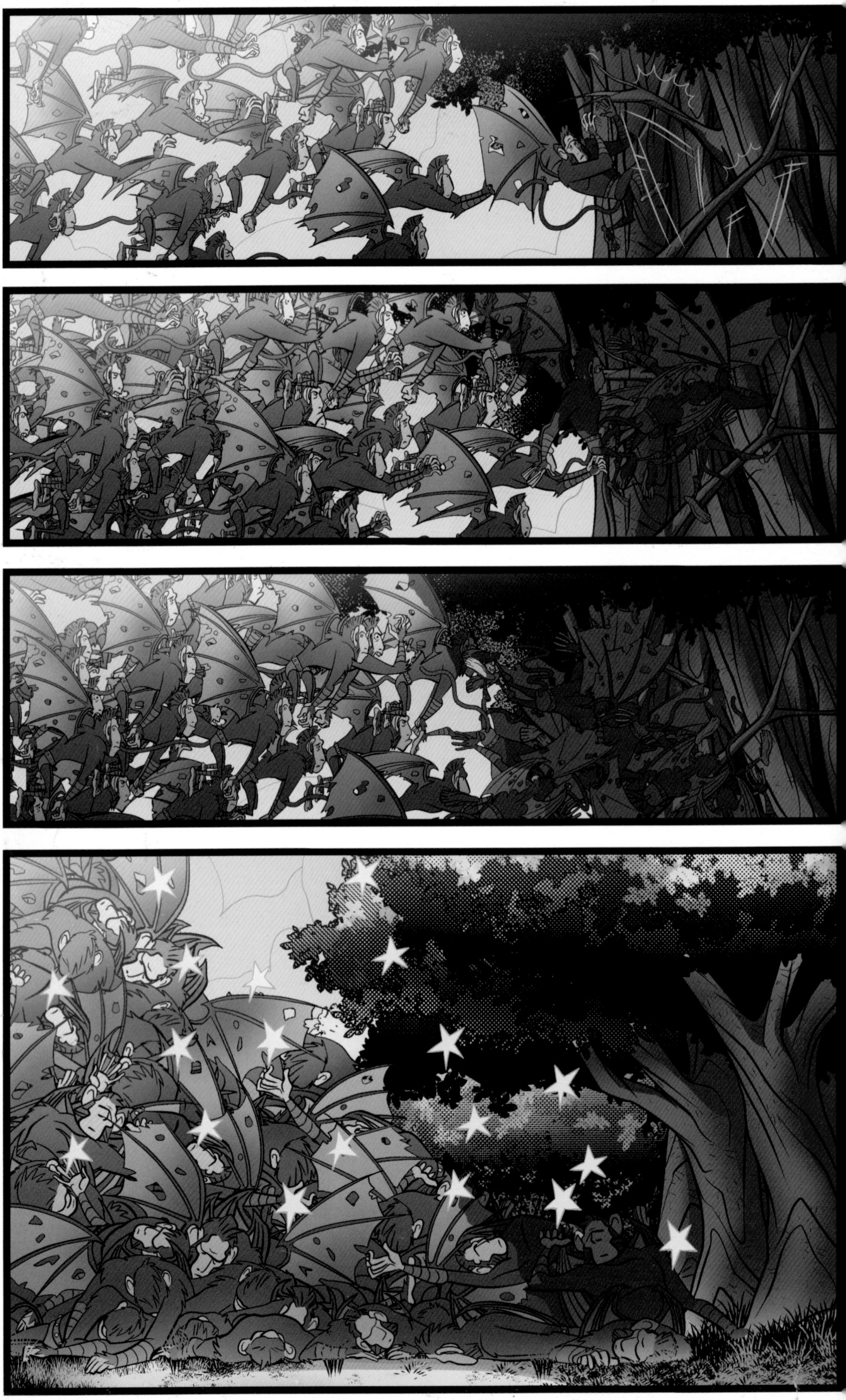

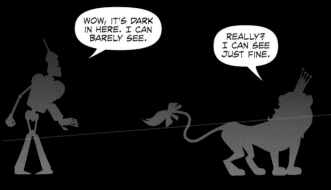

WOW, IT'S DARK IN HERE. I CAN BARELY SEE.

REALLY? I CAN SEE JUST FINE.

THAT'S BECAUSE YOU'RE A CAT, LION. YOU HAVE SUPERIOR NIGHT VISION.

WHAT THE HECK'S A CAT-LION?

NIGHT VISION: ENGAGED
PATHFINDING MODE: ON

LION
(BIGCATUS COURAGEOUS)

NEVER MIND... LET'S SEE...

scOS
• BRAIN POWER: 100%
• STRAW LEVEL: MIN - REROUTING
• FIRE DANGER: LOW

OOH. I HAVE A LIGHT.

AAH! PUT THAT OUT! I'M GOING TO CATCH FIRE!

AND NOW I CAN'T SEE!

SORRY... SORRY... SO, SORRY.

COME ON. WE CAN LEAD YOU. WE'RE IN THE HOME STRETCH TO THE EMERALD CITY.

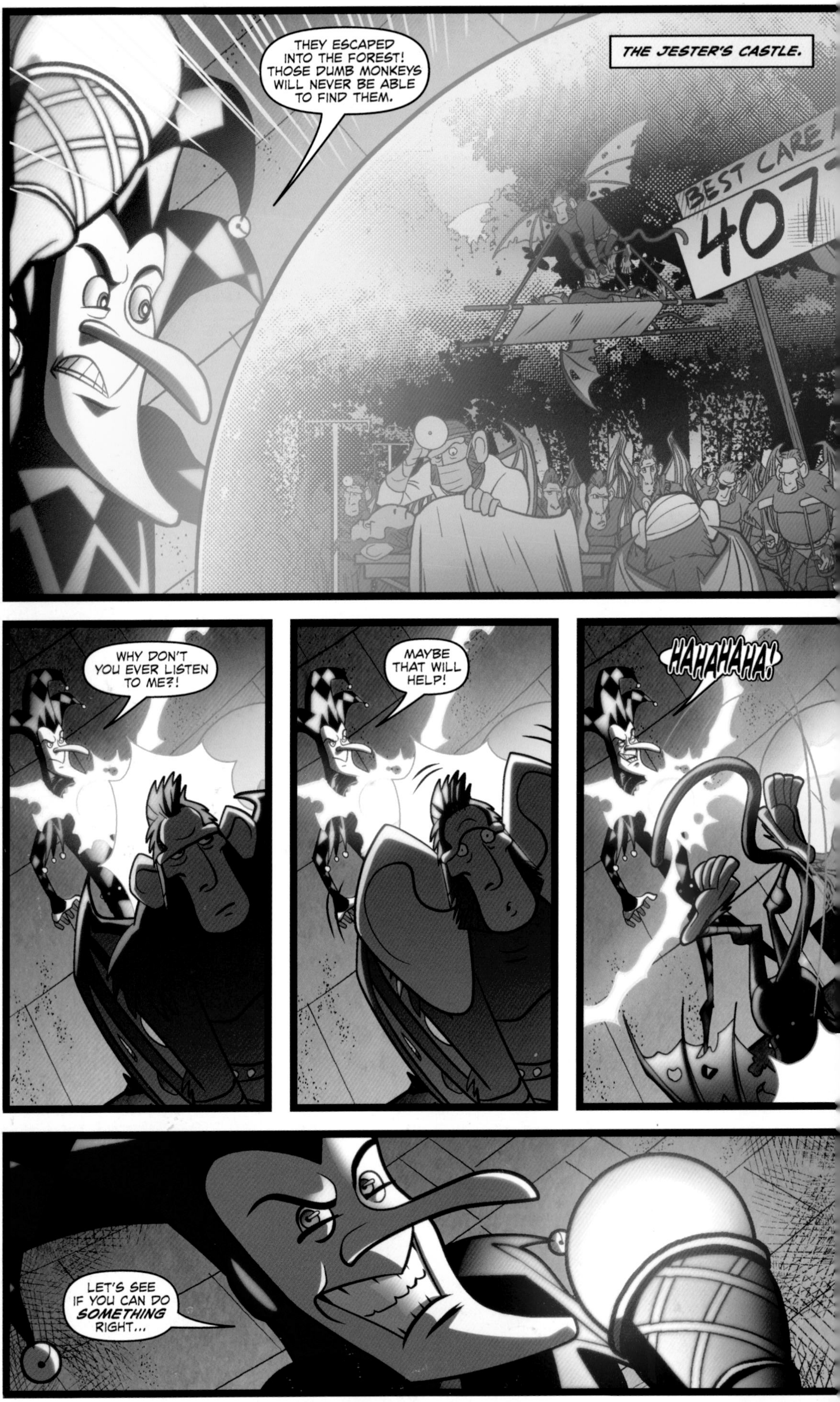
THE JESTER'S CASTLE.
THEY ESCAPED INTO THE FOREST! THOSE DUMB MONKEYS WILL NEVER BE ABLE TO FIND THEM.
BEST CARE
407
WHY DON'T YOU EVER LISTEN TO ME?!
MAYBE THAT WILL HELP!
HAHAHAHA!
LET'S SEE IF YOU CAN DO SOMETHING RIGHT...

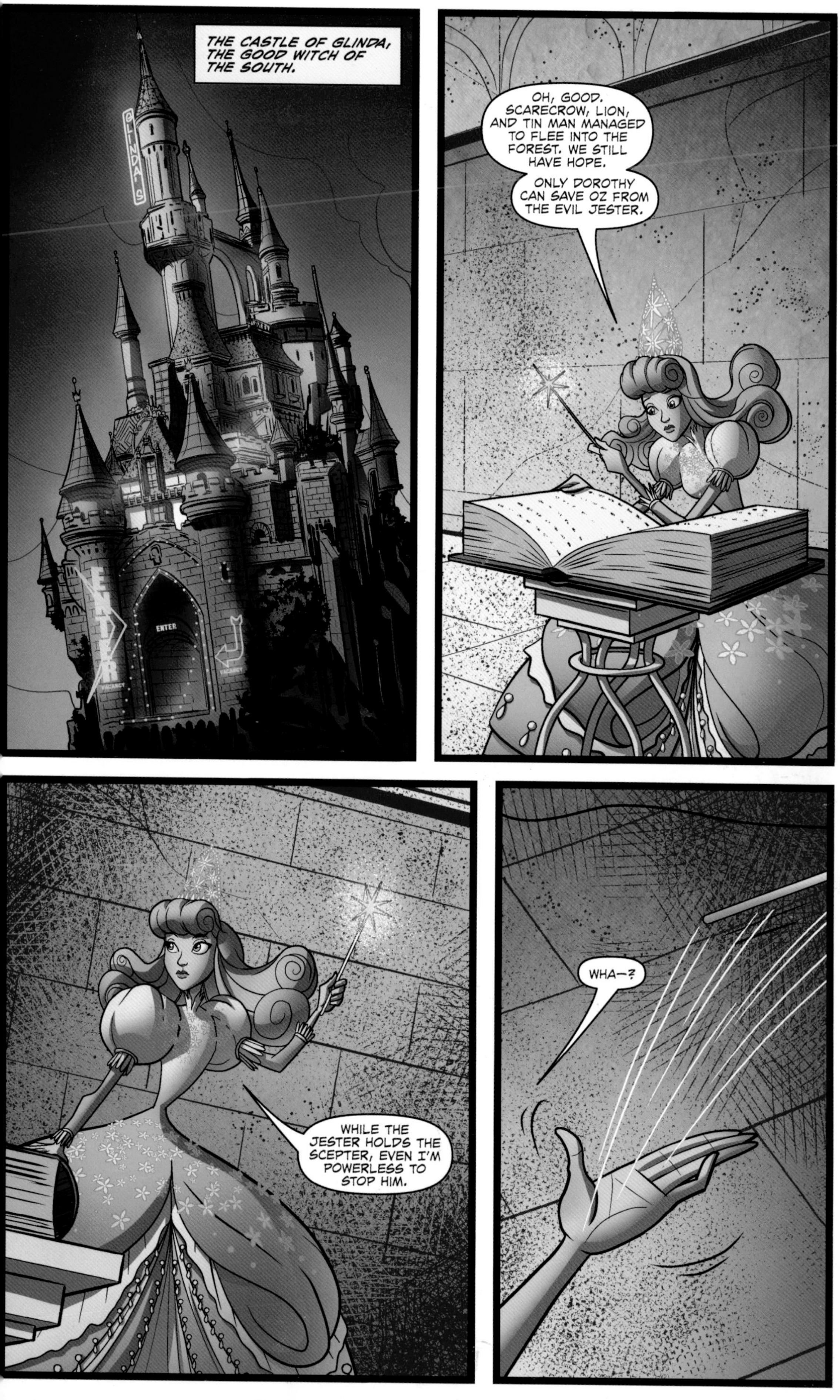
THE CASTLE OF GLINDA, THE GOOD WITCH OF THE SOUTH.
GLINDA'S
ENTER
ENTER
VACANCY
VACANCY
OH, GOOD. SCARECROW, LION, AND TIN MAN MANAGED TO FLEE INTO THE FOREST. WE STILL HAVE HOPE.
ONLY DOROTHY CAN SAVE OZ FROM THE EVIL JESTER.
WHILE THE JESTER HOLDS THE SCEPTER, EVEN I'M POWERLESS TO STOP HIM.
WHA—?

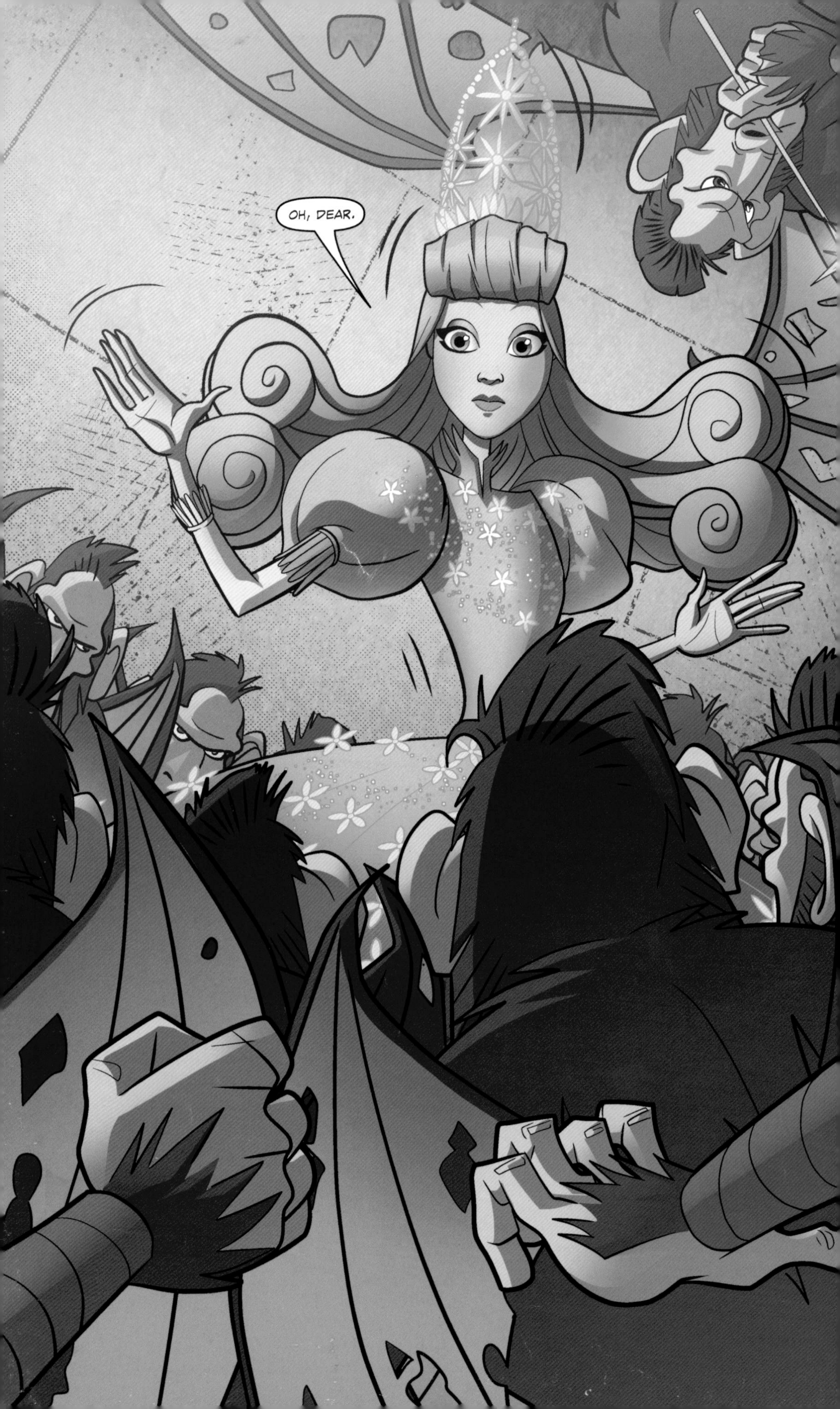
OH, DEAR.

THE EMERALD CITY.

I KNOW I SAW THAT PRISM AROUND HERE SOMEWHERE...

EUREKA!

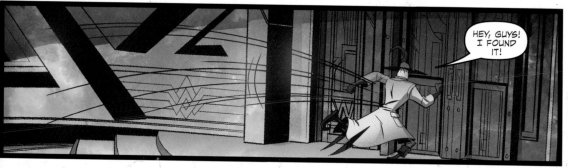

HEY, GUYS! I FOUND IT!

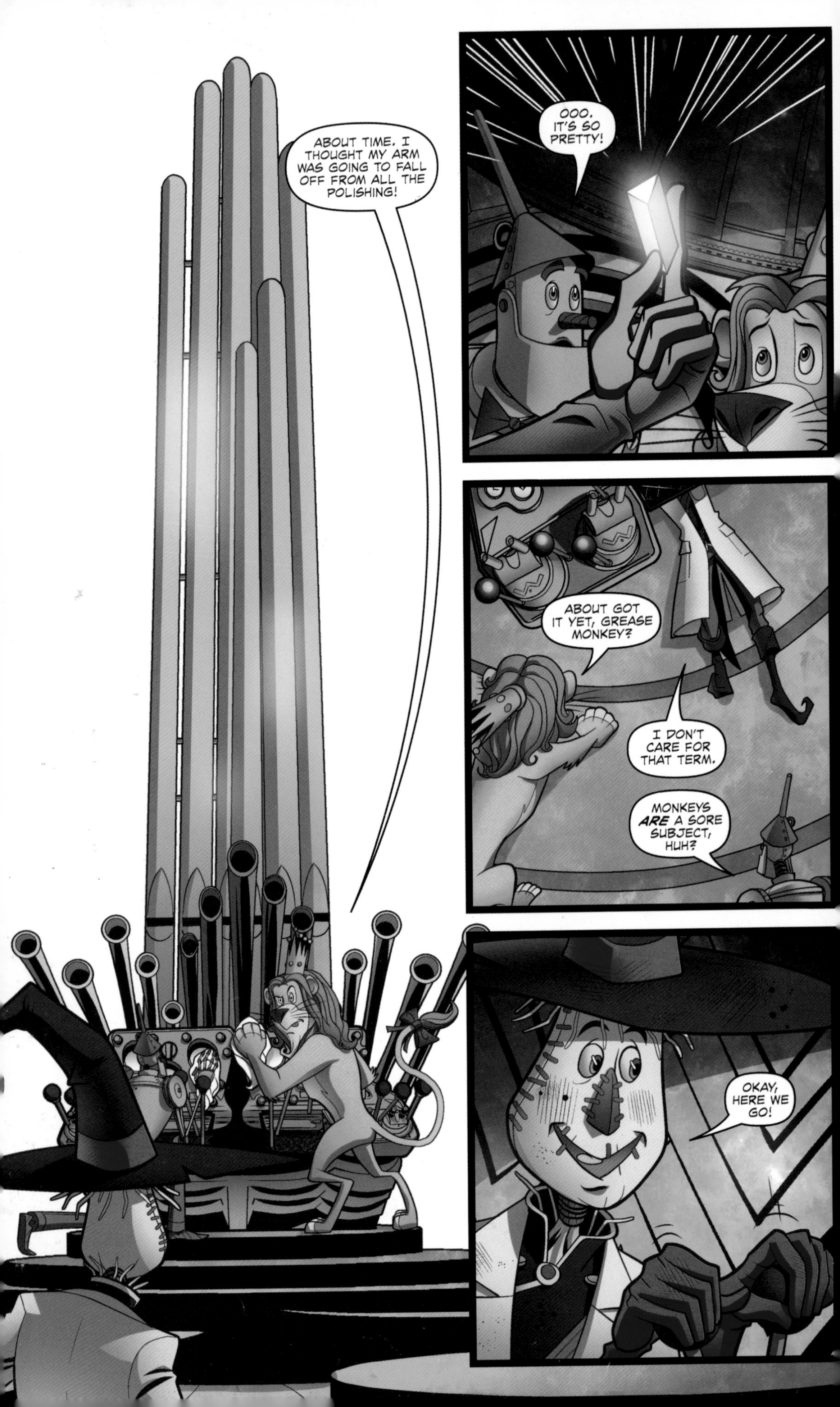
ABOUT TIME. I THOUGHT MY ARM WAS GOING TO FALL OFF FROM ALL THE POLISHING!
OOO. IT'S SO PRETTY!
ABOUT GOT IT YET, GREASE MONKEY?
I DON'T CARE FOR THAT TERM.
MONKEYS **ARE** A SORE SUBJECT, HUH?
OKAY, HERE WE GO!

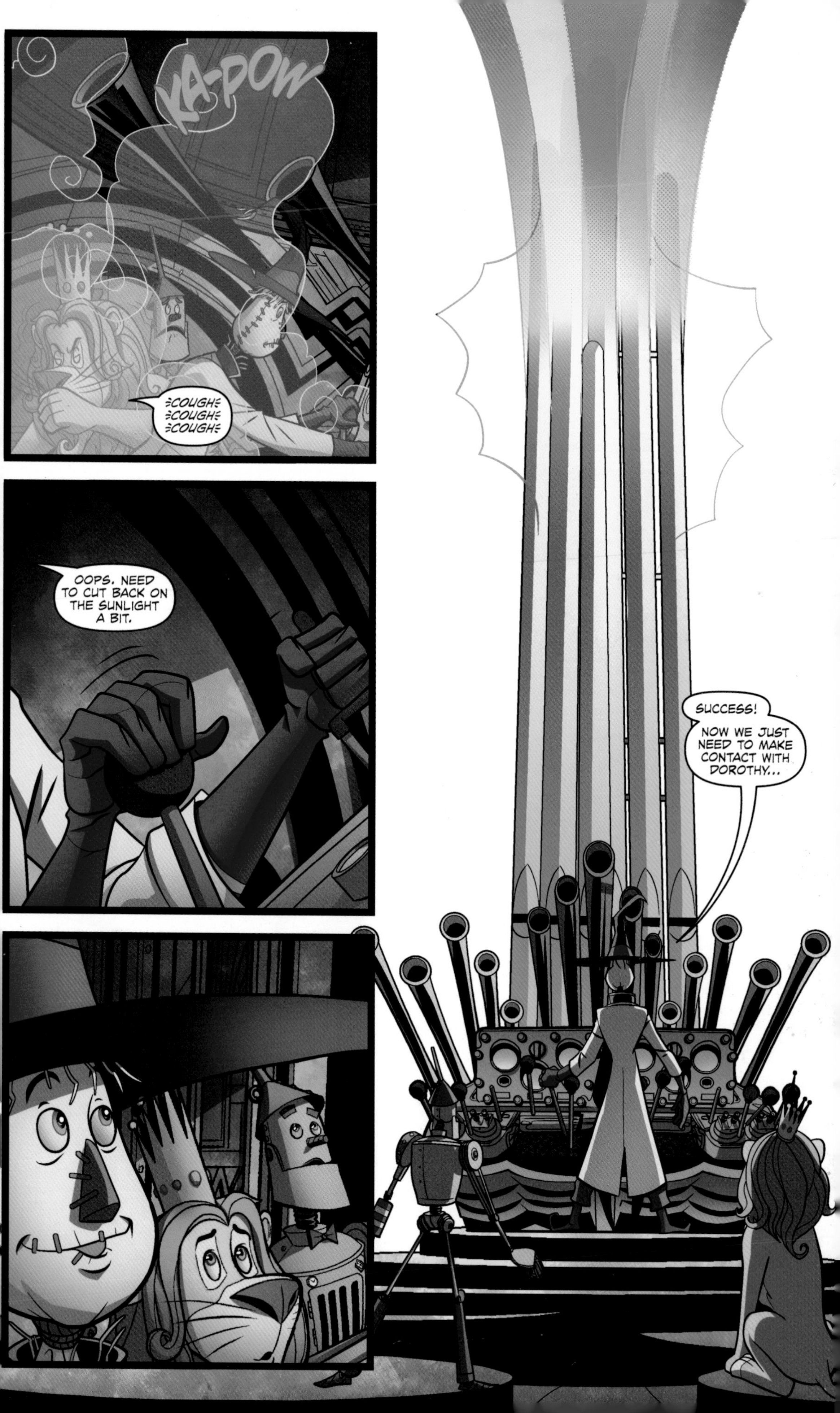
KA-POW
COUGH COUGH COUGH
OOPS. NEED TO CUT BACK ON THE SUNLIGHT A BIT.
SUCCESS!
NOW WE JUST NEED TO MAKE CONTACT WITH DOROTHY...

"...AND TRANSPORT HER HERE FROM KANSAS."

HONK HONK HONK

WILL THESE HICKS JUST GET OUT OF MY WAY ALREADY?!

SINCE WE'RE RUNNING THESE PEOPLE OUT OF THEIR HOMES, THE LEAST THEY CAN DO IS *RUN*.

YOU REALLY SHOULD BUY YOURSELF A SENSE OF HUMOR.

NOW, LET'S SEE THE NEXT HOUSE TO CONDEMN...

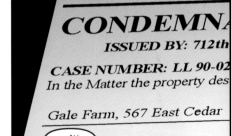

CONDEMNA

ISSUED BY: 712th

CASE NUMBER: LL 90-02
In the Matter the property des

Gale Farm, 567 East Cedar

...AH, THE GALE FARM...

TO   TERED   ERTY

Henry Gale

Affidavits by   e Court
unsafe and/o   e due to th

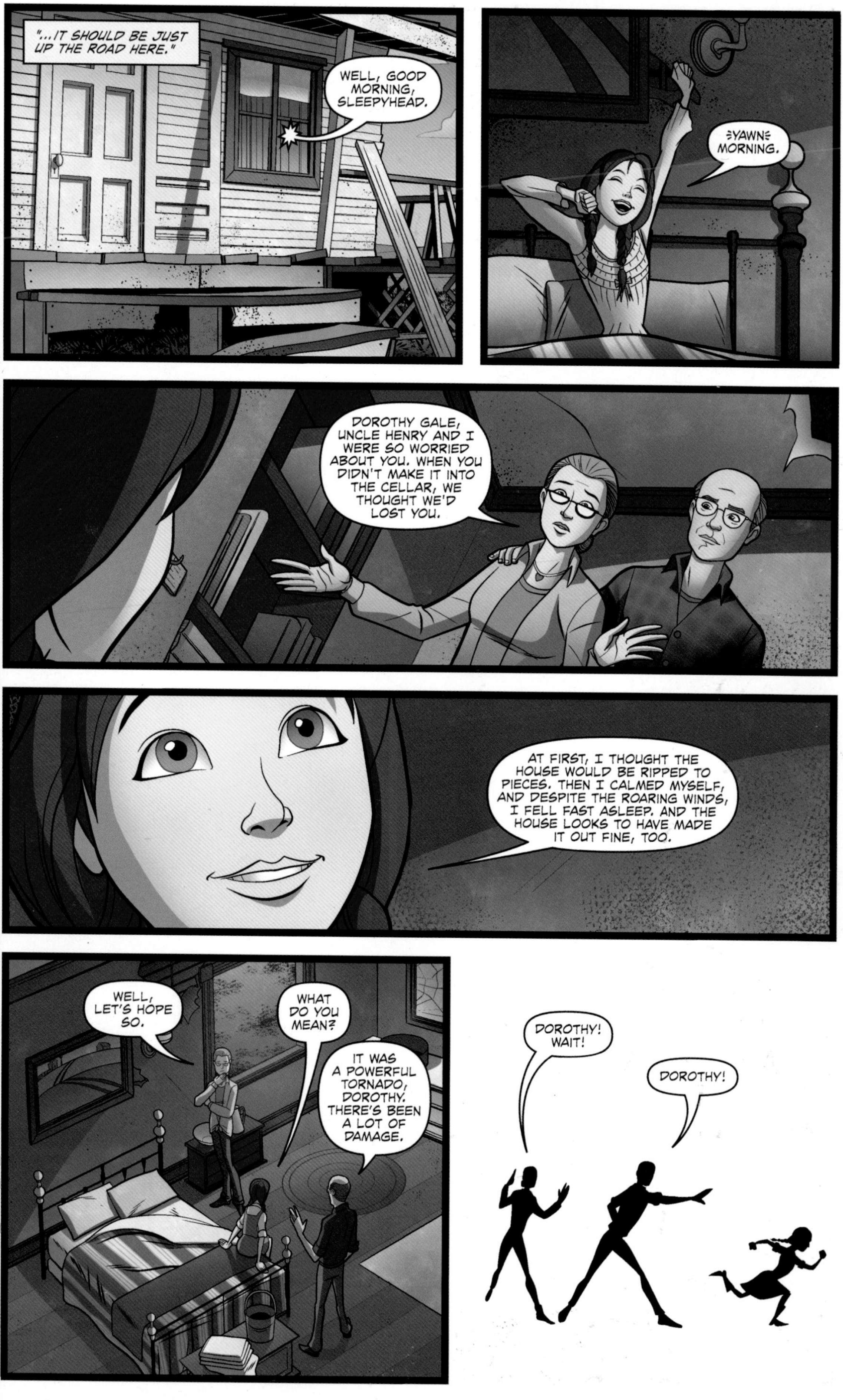
"...IT SHOULD BE JUST UP THE ROAD HERE."
WELL, GOOD MORNING, SLEEPYHEAD.
=YAWN= MORNING.
DOROTHY GALE, UNCLE HENRY AND I WERE SO WORRIED ABOUT YOU. WHEN YOU DIDN'T MAKE IT INTO THE CELLAR, WE THOUGHT WE'D LOST YOU.
AT FIRST, I THOUGHT THE HOUSE WOULD BE RIPPED TO PIECES. THEN I CALMED MYSELF, AND DESPITE THE ROARING WINDS, I FELL FAST ASLEEP. AND THE HOUSE LOOKS TO HAVE MADE IT OUT FINE, TOO.
WELL, LET'S HOPE SO.
WHAT DO YOU MEAN?
IT WAS A POWERFUL TORNADO, DOROTHY. THERE'S BEEN A LOT OF DAMAGE.
DOROTHY! WAIT!
DOROTHY!

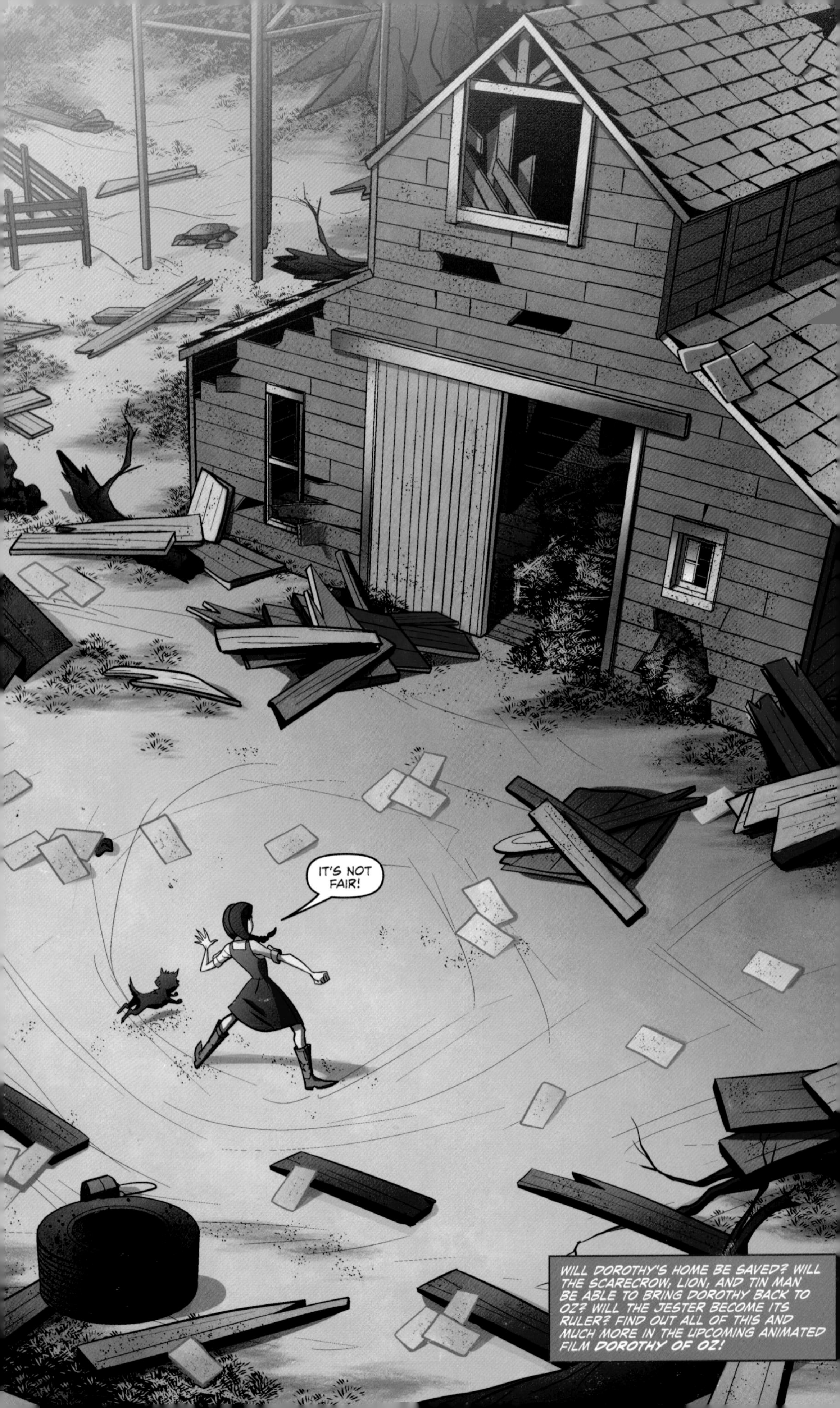
IT'S NOT FAIR!
WILL DOROTHY'S HOME BE SAVED? WILL THE SCARECROW, LION, AND TIN MAN BE ABLE TO BRING DOROTHY BACK TO OZ? WILL THE JESTER BECOME ITS RULER? FIND OUT ALL OF THIS AND MUCH MORE IN THE UPCOMING ANIMATED FILM DOROTHY OF OZ!

Cover Gallery

Art by
Eric Shanower

Colors by
Joana Lafuente

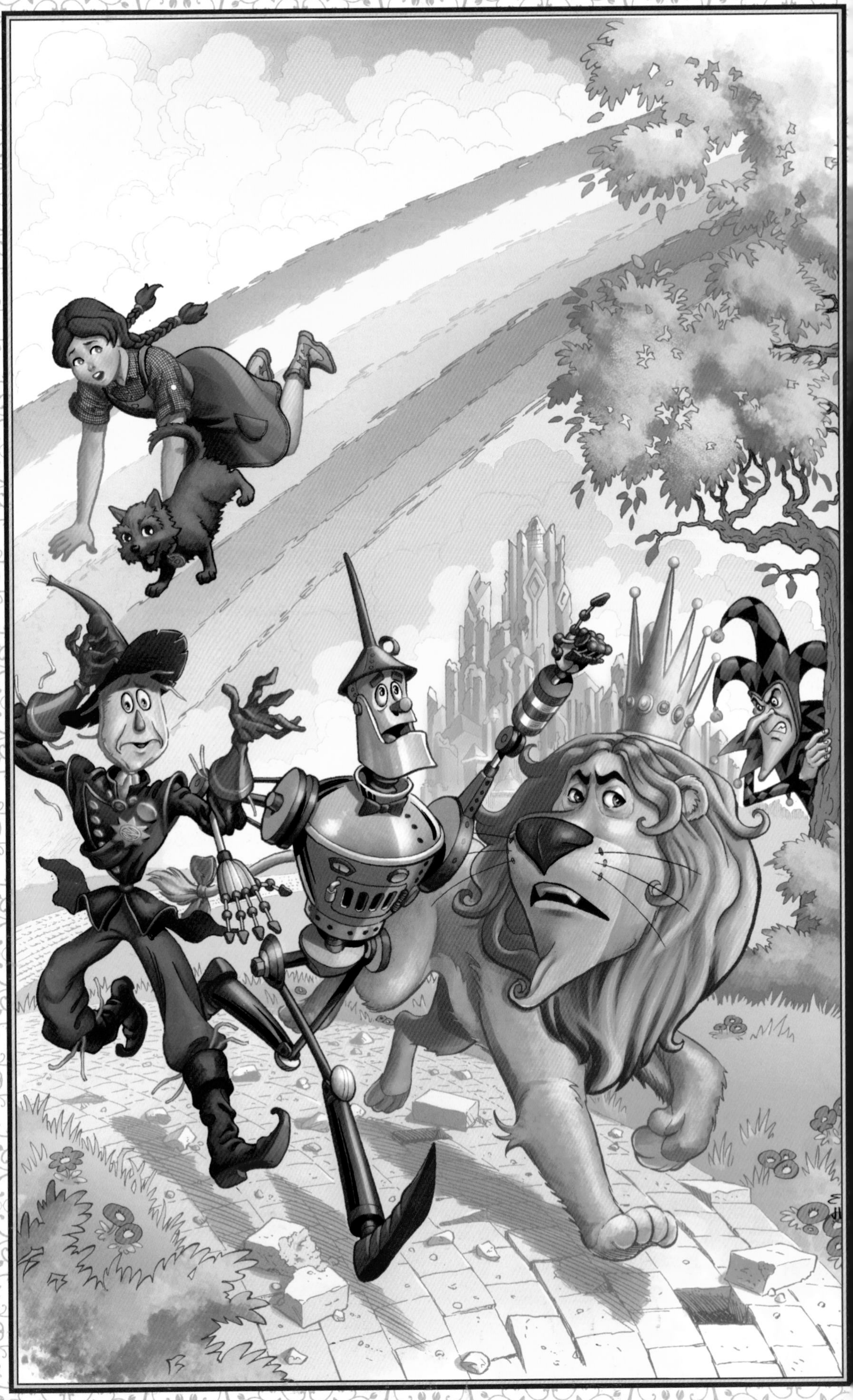

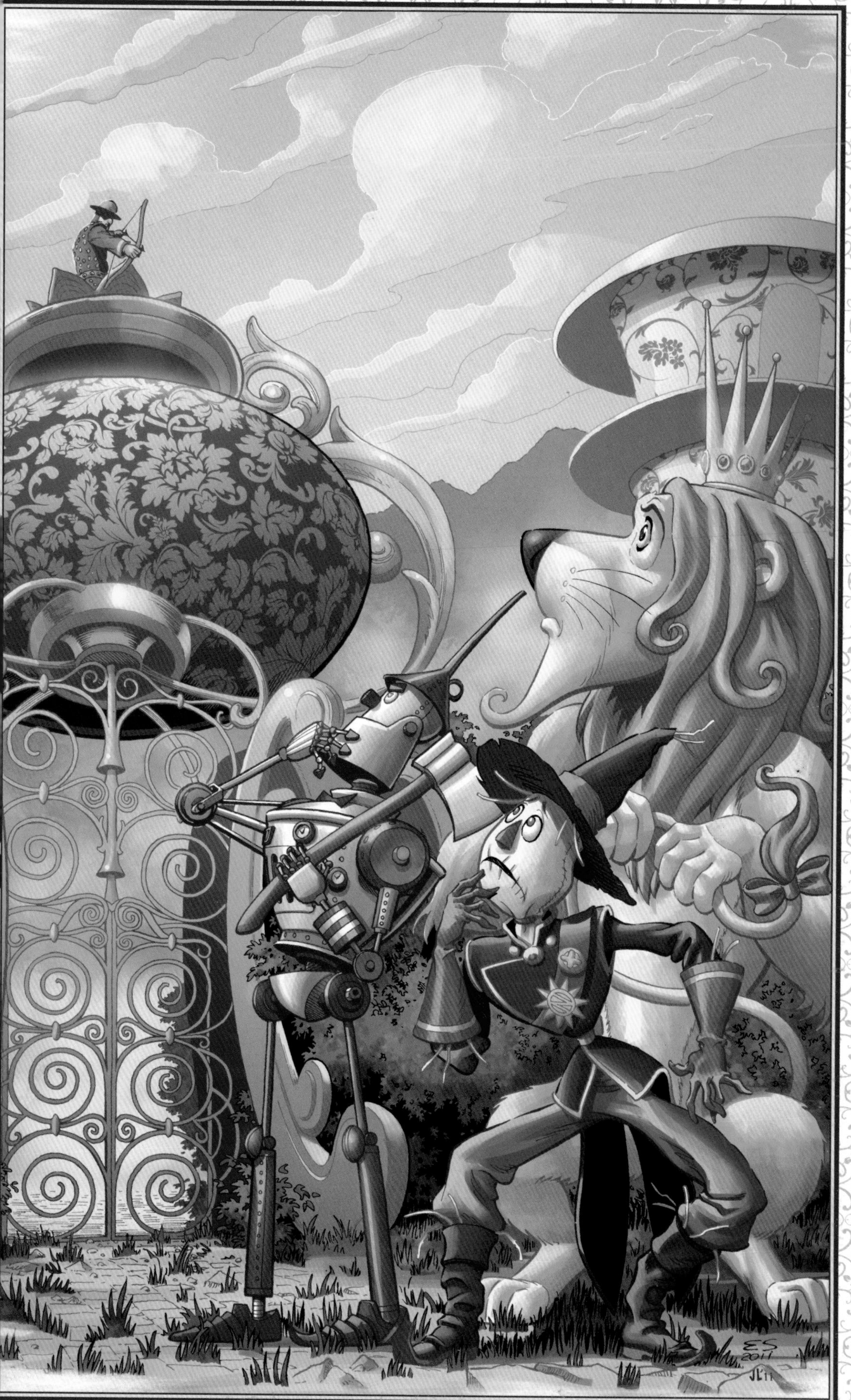

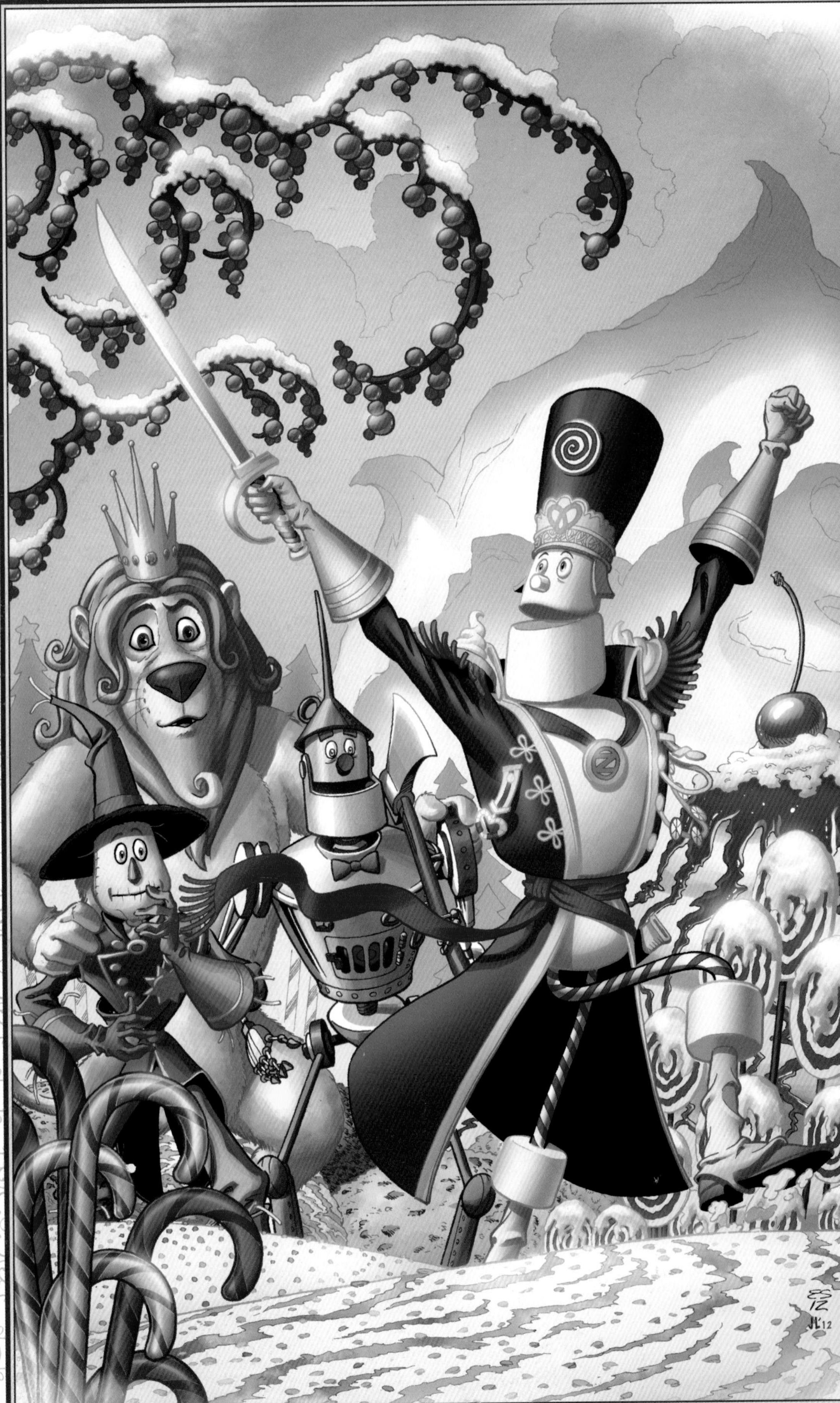

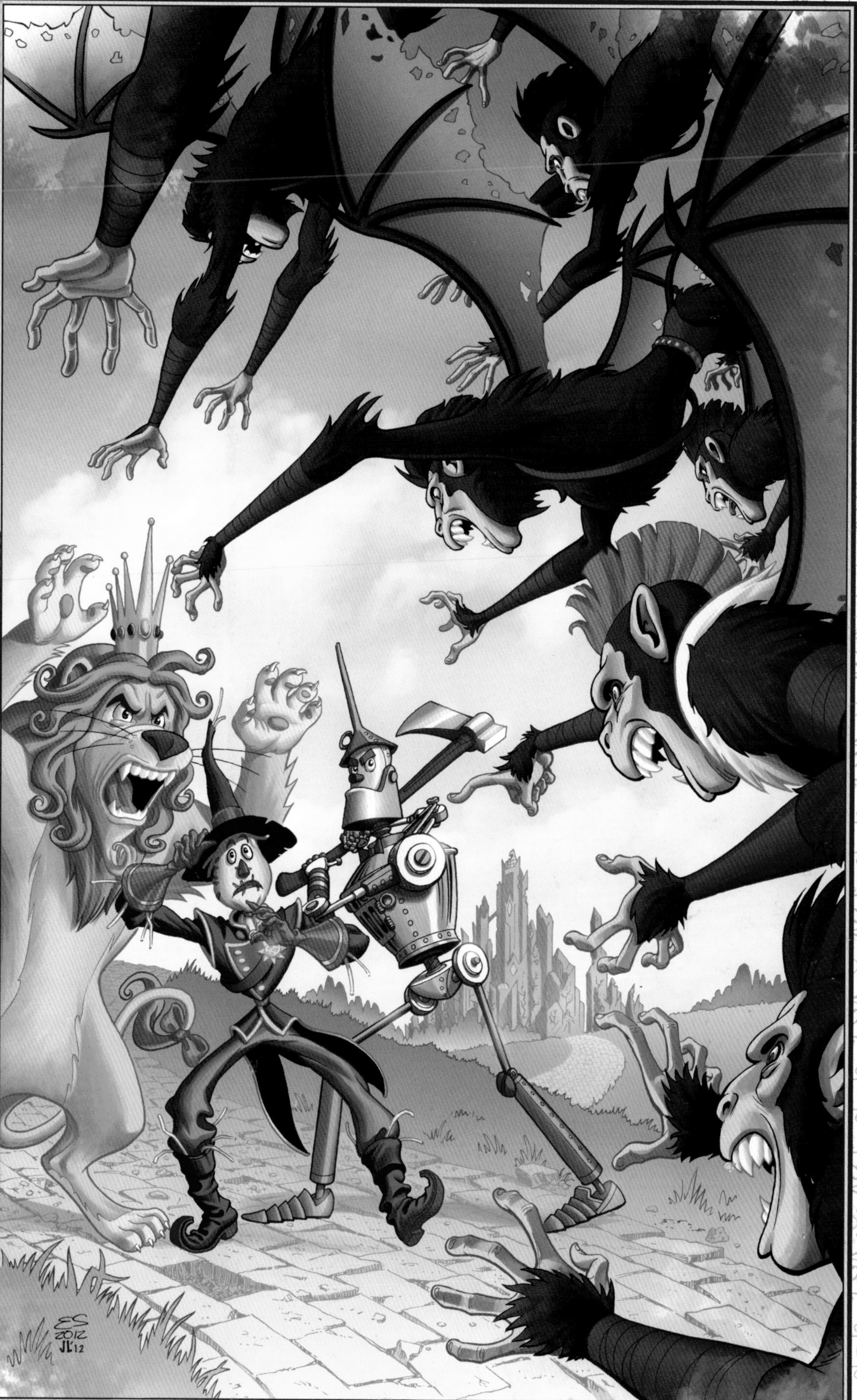

❧ CGI Cover Gallery ❧

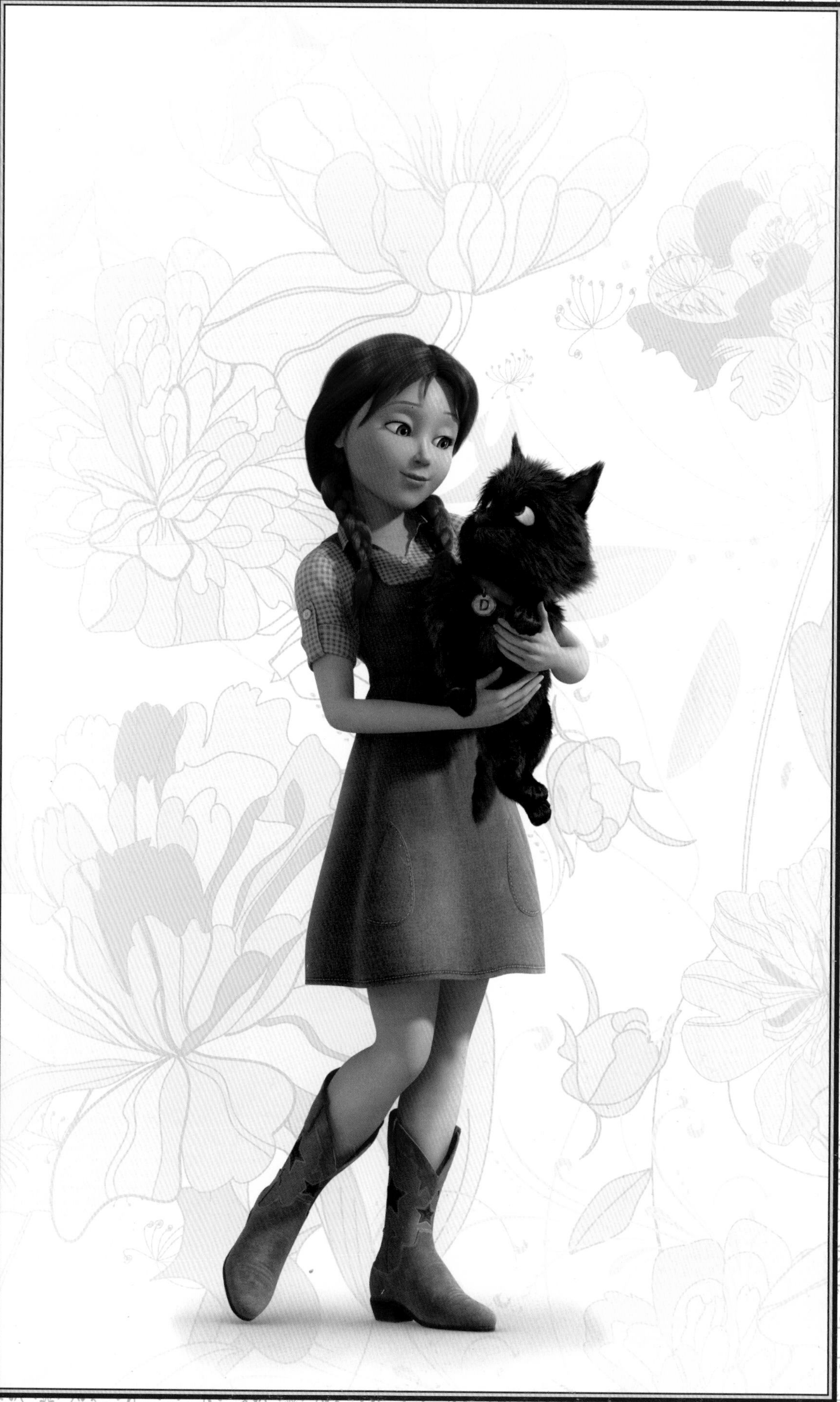

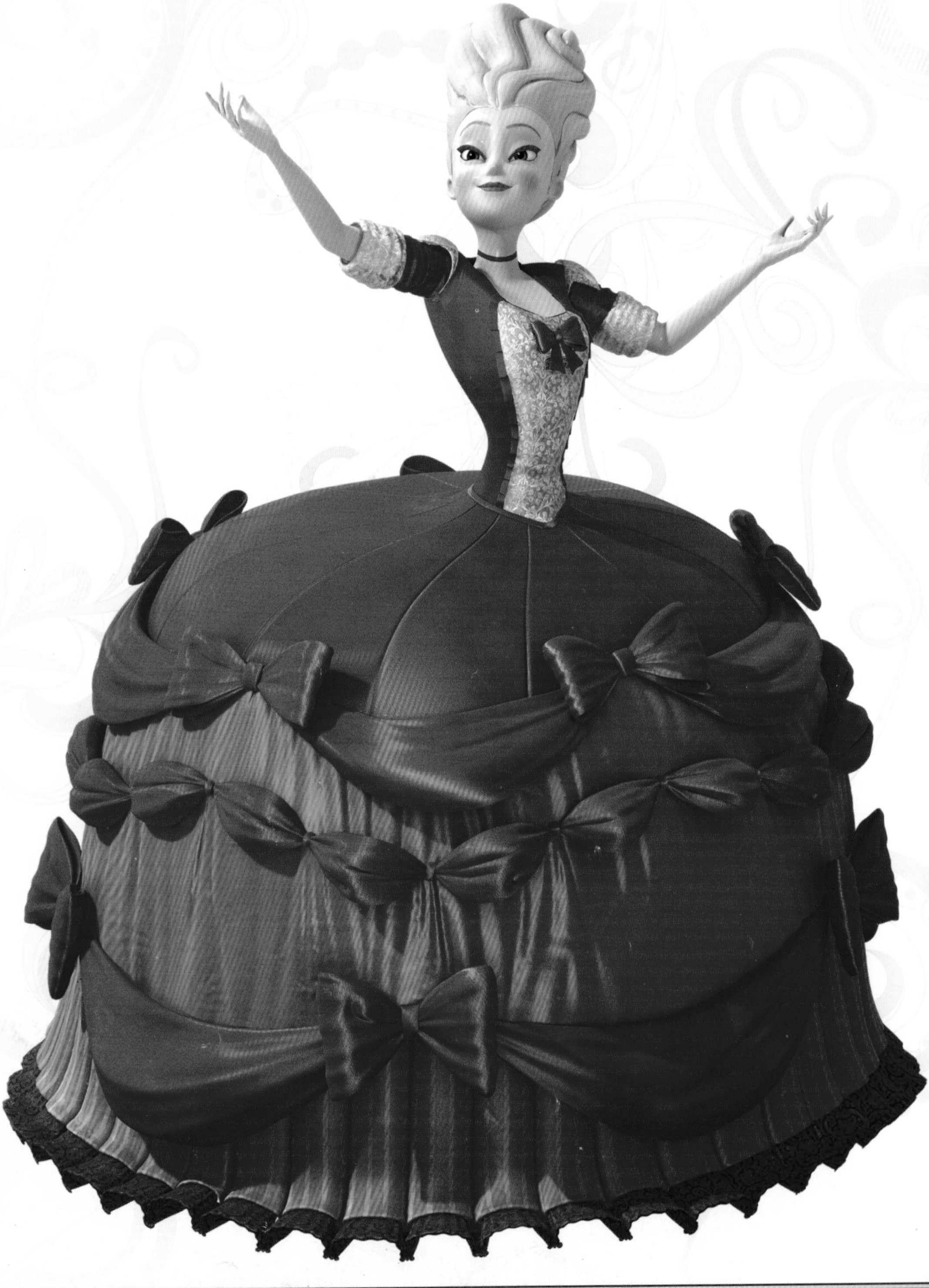

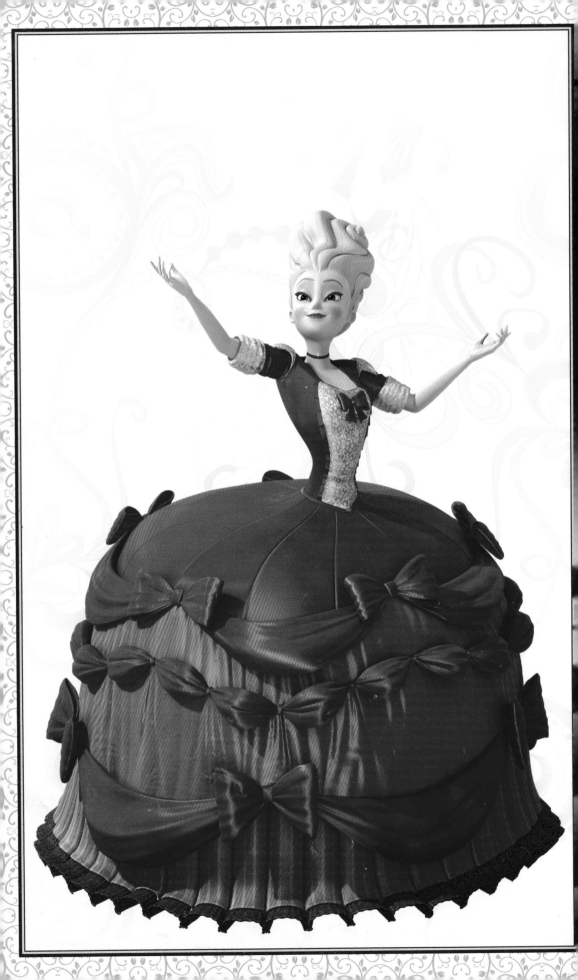

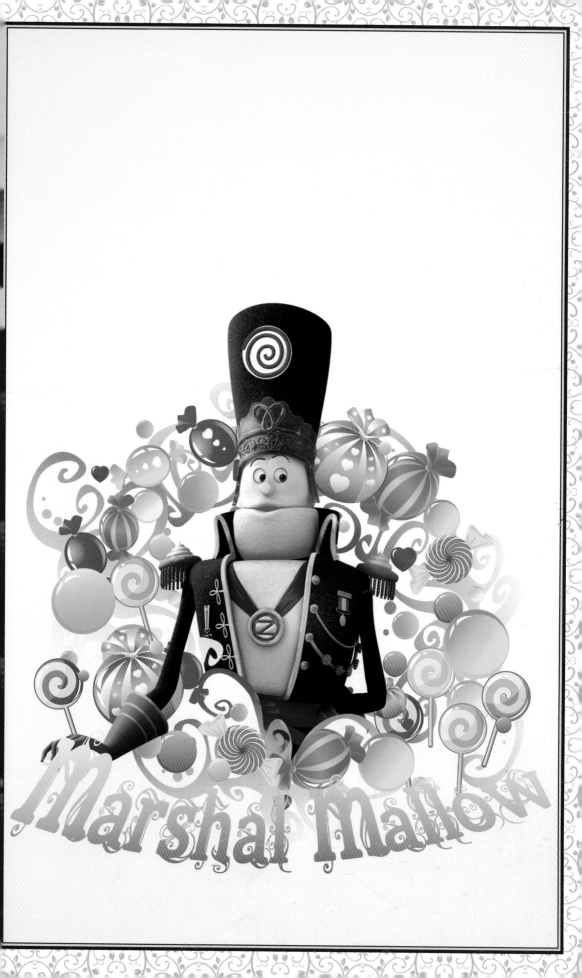

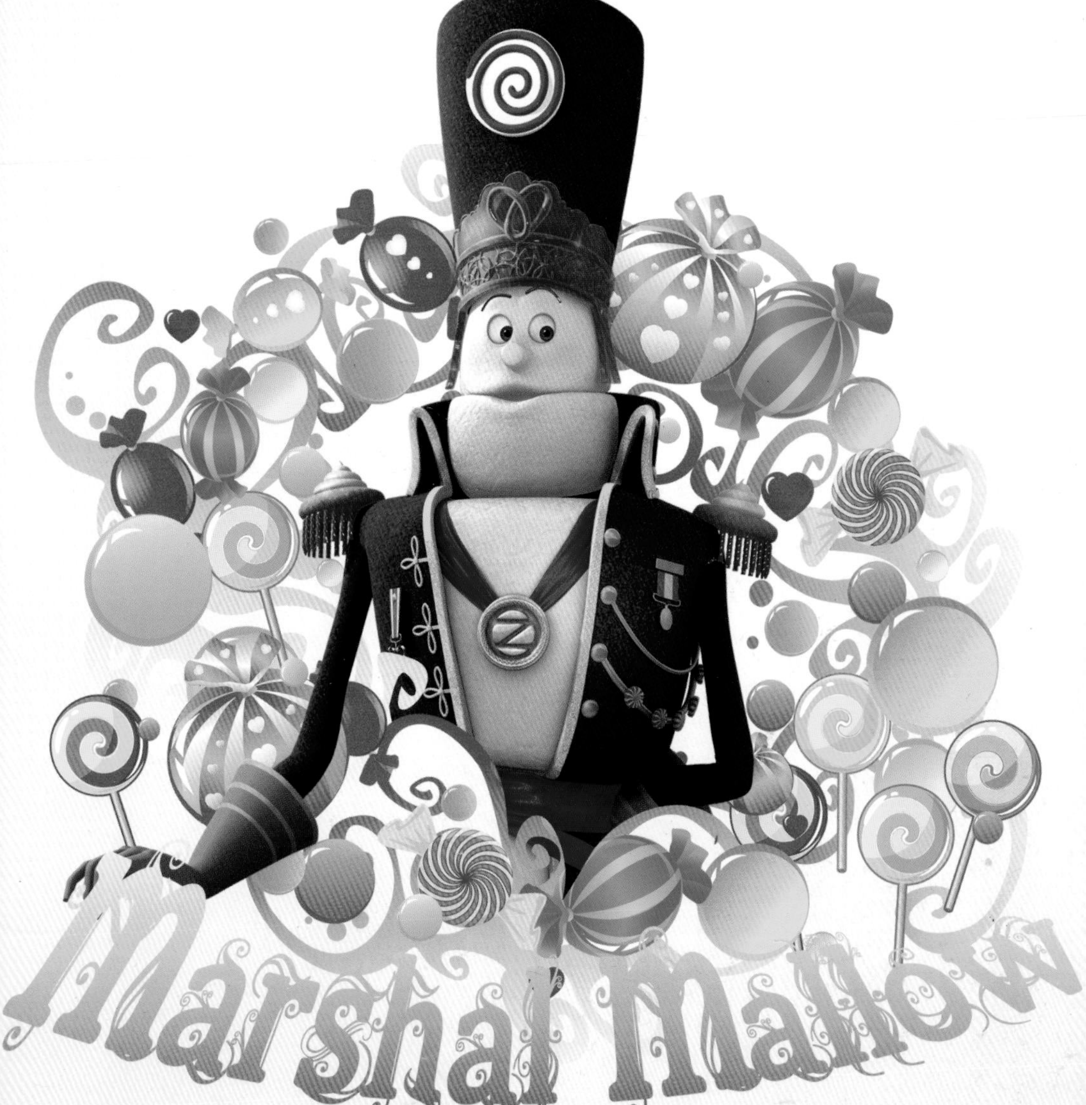
Marshal Mallow

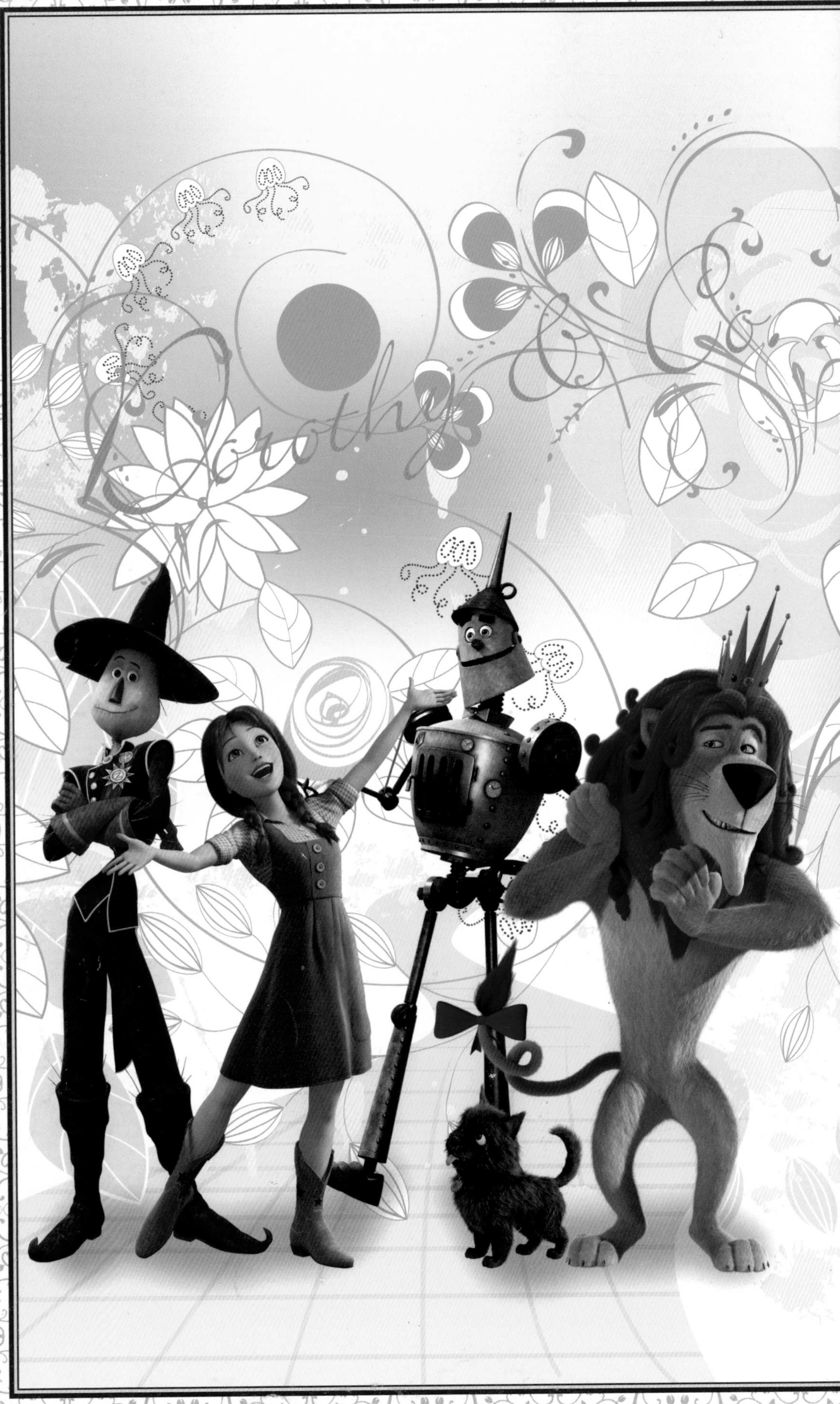
Dorothy & Co.

DOROTHY of OZ™ Prequel

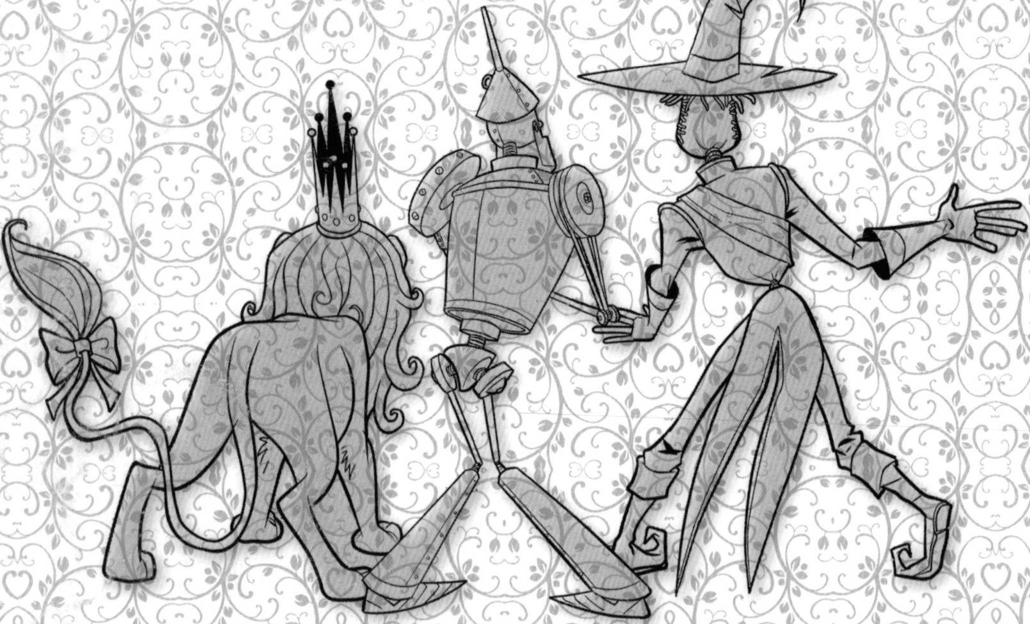

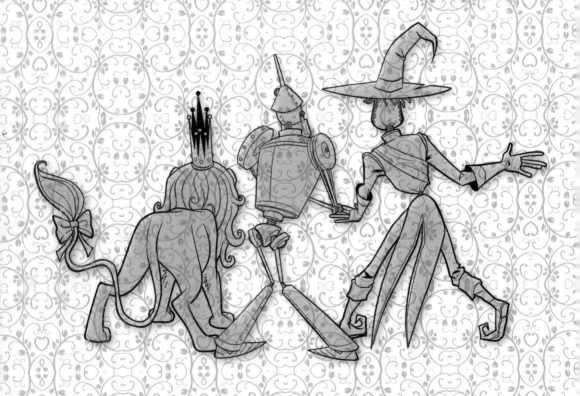